Ready, Set, Promote!

The Essential Marketing and Selling Guide for
Self-Published Authors

VERONICA GOLDSPIEL

Copyright © 2026 by Veronica Goldspiel

Book Cover design: Zeljka Vukojević

Interior design: Veronica Goldspiel

1st Edition 2026

ISBN (Paperback): 979-8-9951232-0-0

Printed in the United States of America

Write It. Finish It. Publish It.

If you picked up ***Ready, Set, Promote***, you're not just hoping your book will sell—you're ready to get it into the hands of readers.

The truth is, book marketing can feel overwhelming—not because you're not capable, but because there's so much conflicting advice and pressure to "do everything."

That's exactly why I created the ***From Writer to Author Newsletter***: a warm, supportive resource to help you stay focused, encouraged, and moving forward with clear, practical writing, publishing, and marketing guidance you can actually use.

When you subscribe, you'll get:

- Real-life strategies to increase visibility and reach more readers

- Simple, effective marketing tips you can implement right away

- Guidance to help you promote your book without feeling pushy or overwhelmed

You don't have to figure this out alone—and you don't have to do it perfectly. You just have to keep showing up and taking the next step.

Subscribe below:

https://goldspiel-creative-enterprises.kit.com/newsletter

Contents

Introduction

Promotion Is a Skill, Not a Personality Trait

Publishing a book is an accomplishment. Promoting it—*successfully*—is an entirely different skill set.

If you're holding this book (or reading it on a screen), chances are you've already crossed one of the hardest milestones in self-publishing: you finished your book and put it into the world. That alone puts you ahead of most people who say they want to be authors.

But once the book is live, the celebration tends to be short-lived. The questions start almost immediately.

Now what?

How do I get people to notice this?

Do I really need ads?

Why does everyone else seem to know something I don't?

I've been there. Repeatedly.

I've published twelve books, including this one, and every single time I release a new title, I learn something new—sometimes because something works, sometimes because something absolutely doesn't.

Self-publishing is not a finish line; it's a moving target. Platforms change. Reader behavior changes. Strategies that worked two years ago quietly stop working. And the truth is, no one ever fully "graduates" from learning how to promote books.

That's one of the reasons I wrote *Ready, Set, Promote.*

This book isn't written from the perspective of a marketing guru who's never struggled to sell a copy. It's written by a self-published author who has launched books, watched rankings climb and fall, tried strategies that paid off, and wasted time (and money) on others that sounded promising but delivered very little. I've felt the excitement of a strong launch—and the frustration of wondering why a good book isn't getting the visibility it deserves.

I wrote this book for you—but I also wrote it for myself.

Because promotion isn't something you "figure out once." It's something you refine with every book you publish.

Promotion Is Not Optional—But It Doesn't Have To Be Expensive

One of the biggest myths in self-publishing is that successful book promotion requires deep pockets and nonstop ads. Amazon ads. Facebook ads. BookBub ads. More ads. Better ads. Bigger budgets.

While paid advertising can (and does) work, it's not the only path—and for many authors, it's not even the *best* one, especially early on.

This book focuses on **proven, low-cost and no-cost strategies**, with a heavy emphasis on **organic visibility**, reader trust, and long-term momentum.

Not hacks. Not gimmicks. Not "go viral overnight" fantasies.

Real strategies that authors can use repeatedly—whether they're publishing their first book or their fifteenth.

Where This Book Fits In Your Publishing Journey

The first book in my Writers & Authors Series, *Ready, Set, Publish,* was about getting your book ready for release.

Now this second book in the series, *Ready, Set, Promote,* is about what happens after your book is published.

This is the part of the process where many authors stall—not because their book isn't good, but because they don't know what to prioritize next.

This book is designed to remove that uncertainty by walking you through everything authors need to consider once their book is live, including:

- Choosing an effective official launch date

- Building and managing a launch team

- Tracking rankings and understanding what they really mean

- Selling books without relying on paid ads

- Organic promotion strategies that compound over time

- Hiring promoters and knowing what to expect

- Keeping your book visible long after launch week ends

- And why writing your next book is often the smartest marketing move you can make

Promotion isn't a single event. It's an ongoing process—and the authors who succeed are rarely the loudest. They're the ones who show up consistently with a plan.

Experience Without the Pretense of Perfection

This book isn't built on theory alone. It's built on experience—on launches that worked, launches that underperformed, and adjustments made along the way. While I've had measurable success in self-publishing, I don't believe there is a single formula that guarantees results forever.

Anyone who claims otherwise isn't paying attention or is just outright lying.

What *does* work is learning how to evaluate what you're doing, tracking results, repeating what works, and letting go of what doesn't. Promotion becomes far less intimidating when you stop chasing magic answers and start building systems that support your long-term goals as an author.

That's what this book is designed to help you do.

The Long Game (And Why That's Good News)

If you're looking for a one-week launch that guarantees lifetime sales, this probably isn't the book you're looking for.

But if you want to understand how book promotion actually works, how to build visibility over time, and how to make each new release easier to sell than the last, you're in exactly the right place.

One of the most overlooked truths in self-publishing is this: the best way to sell your first book is your second book. And the best way to sell your second book is everything you learn along the way.

Let's get started.

PART I – Pre-Launch Promotion

(Yes, You Still Need This)

Chapter One

Thinking Like a Marketer Without Becoming One

Many authors assume that publishing a book is the final step—that once the book is available, readers will somehow find it. This belief is especially common among self-published authors, and it's one of the most damaging misconceptions in the industry.

The reality is far less romantic and far more competitive.

Each year, an estimated **1.4 million books** are published, with roughly **7,500 new books added to Amazon every single day.** When a self-published author releases a book without any promotion, that book is not entering a marketplace that is waiting for it. It is being dropped into a vast ocean already crowded with content. Without intentional visibility, the book quickly sinks—regardless of its quality.

Marketing, then, is not about manipulation or ego. It's about ensuring that your work has a chance to be seen.

The Difference Between Promotion and Spam

One of the primary reasons authors resist marketing is the fear of being perceived as spammy. This fear often leads to complete inaction, which is far more harmful than imperfect promotion.

Spam is indiscriminate and self-serving. It pushes the same message repeatedly without regard for audience, context, or relevance. Its sole objective is attention.

Promotion is strategic and audience-aware. It's grounded in clarity: who the book is for, what problem it solves, and why it matters. Effective promotion communicates value before it asks for a sale.

When authors explain their book's purpose, share insights related to its content, or educate readers about the issues the book addresses, they are not spamming—they are positioning. Promotion becomes problematic only when it lacks intention or respect for the reader's experience.

Avoiding promotion entirely does not preserve professionalism. It simply removes your book from the conversation.

Selling Books by Being Helpful, Visible, and Consistent

Books sell when readers trust the author behind them. That trust is built over time through three behaviors: being helpful, being visible, and being consistent.

Being **helpful** establishes credibility. Authors who share relevant knowledge, guidance, or perspective demonstrate expertise and build confidence with their audience.

Being **visible** ensures recognition. Readers cannot purchase a book they don't remember or encounter. Visibility doesn't require constant output; it requires intentional presence in spaces where potential readers already exist.

Being **consistent** reinforces reliability. When authors communicate regularly and coherently, readers know what to expect. This reduces friction and increases the likelihood of engagement.

These principles are not theoretical. Authors who publish without promotion often seen initial rankings drop rapidly after launch.

This was the case with my first four books. Despite completing and releasing them, I didn't integrate marketing into the process. As a result, rankings declined quickly, and monthly royalties remained at zero.

Once marketing and promotion became a planned part of the publishing process, the results changed for the better.

Why Authors Who Dislike Marketing Still Need a Plan

Discomfort with marketing doesn't eliminate its necessity. Without a plan, promotion becomes reactive and inconsistent—often driven by urgency or frustration rather than strategy.

A marketing plan provides structure. It allows authors to approach promotion systematically instead of emotionally. With a plan in place, decisions are made in advance, expectations are managed, and effort compounds over time.

The difference between unplanned and strategic promotion is measurable. After integrating marketing into the release and post-launch process for my last six books, sales began to increase steadily. What had previously generated no monthly royalties grew into consistent daily sales. Over time, this resulted in regularly monthly royalties in the range of **$200-300 and it continues to grow.**

This outcome was not the result of viral success or luck. It was the result of planning, execution, and consistency.

A Critical Mindset Shift: Passion and Profit Are Not Opposites

One of the most persistent misconceptions among writers is that marketing, promotion, or earning money somehow diminishes the integrity of the work. Many believe that "real" writers write purely for passion, and that financial reward implies selling out.

This belief is not only inaccurate—it is extremely limiting.

Writing with passion and earning income are not mutually exclusive. Recognition, readership, and financial reward are not betrayals of creative intent; they are outcomes of it. A book that is never discovered cannot create impact, no matter how meaningful its message.

If you invested months or years into writing a book, it's reasonable—and responsible—to want it to be read. Promotion is not about compromising values. It's about honoring the work by giving it the opportunity to reach its audience.

Marketing reframed this way is not self-centered. It's reader-centered.

Invitation, Not Interruption

At its core, promotion is an invitation. It informs readers that a resource exists and allows them to decide whether it's relevant to them.

You are not responsible for persuading everyone. You are responsible for clarity and visibility. When authors understand this distinction, marketing becomes a professional practice rather than a personal discomfort.

Your role is to make your book findable. The reader's role is to choose.

Chapter Two

Choosing Your Official Launch Date (and Why It Matters)

A book launch is not simply a date on the calendar. It's a time-based marketing event, and its success depends heavily on when and how attention is concentrated. Authors who treat launch timing casually often limit their book's potential before promotion even begins.

Choosing an effective launch date requires understanding reader behavior, attention patterns, and the mechanics of coordinated promotion.

Why "Publish Date" and "Launch Date" Are Not the Same

The **publish date** is the day a book becomes available for purchase. The **launch date** is the period when promotion is intentionally focused on driving visibility and engagement.

These two dates should be treated as separate decisions.

Publishing a book quietly before launching allows retailer systems time to index the title, populate categories, and display metadata correctly. It also provides space to gather early reviews and ensure that purchase links function as expected.

Launching without this preparation often leads to missed opportunities. Attention is directed toward a book that may not yet be fully supported by the platform infrastructure that influences discoverability.

Publishing makes the book available. Launching activates demand.

Best Days of the Week to Launch

From both industry data and practical experience, weekday launches consistently outperform weekend launches for most books.

People are more likely to check email, browse online, and respond to marketing messages during the workweek. Weekends and holidays, while seemingly convenient, often result in delayed or reduced engagement. Readers are traveling, celebrating, or spending time away from their devices.

Because a launch is time-sensitive, delayed responses can significantly weaken results. When readers see a message days later, momentum has already passed. This reduces the effectiveness or coordinated promotion and can lead to disappointing outcomes—not because of the book, but because of the timing.

For this reason, most of my book launches are scheduled midweek, and I avoid weekends and holidays unless the book's subject matter directly aligns with that period.

Timing Your Launch

Timing decisions should always account for the broader calendar.

Holidays, seasonal transitions, and cultural events influence how readers allocate attention. Launching during a high-distraction period often means competing with forces far stronger than your marketing efforts.

That said, seasonality is not fixed. Engagement patters vary depending on genre, topic, and audience.

Some books perform better at certain times of the year, while others are less affected by seasonality. These patterns can also shift over time.

The key is awareness. Authors who plan launches without considering seasonal context risk working against natural reader behavior instead of leveraging it.

Strategic timing doesn't guarantee success, but poor timing can significantly reduce the effectiveness of an otherwise strong launch.

Maximizing Your Launch Across Platforms

A launch is most effective when promotion is concentrated into a defined window rather than spread thing over time.

All of my book launches follow a clearly defined launch period—typically a two-day window—where promotional efforts are focused and coordinated. This concentrated approach creates urgency and reinforces visibility across platforms.

When readers encounter consistent messaging within a short time frame—via email, social media, or other channels—they are more likely to act. When promotion is fragmented or inconsistent, attention dissipates.

Coordination ensures that each platform supports the same objective at the same time. This alignment amplifies results without requiring excessive promotion.

Deciding When *Your* Launch Should Be

While best practices and data provide useful guidance, there is no single "correct" launch date for every author.

The most effective launch is one that aligns with your audience, your availability, and your capacity to promote consistently during the launch window.

Before choosing a launch date, authors should ask themselves several practical questions:

- When will my audience be most attentive and reachable?

- Are there holidays, major events, or seasonal distractions that could compete for attention?

- Do I have enough time in the days surrounding the launch to actively promote and engage?

- Am I launching multiple books or projects close together that could dilute focus?

- Do I have the marketing assets prepared in advance (email content, social posts, links, graphics)?

The purpose of those questions is not to create hesitation, but to ensure that the launch is supported rather than rushed. A well-timed launch increases the likelihood that readers will see, process, and respond to your messaging within the intended window.

Choosing the Length of Your Launch Window

Launches don't need to follow a single format.

As I said earlier in this chapter, I almost always use a **two-day launch window**, concentrating promotional efforts into a short, focused period. This approach works well because it creates urgency while remaining manageable and repeatable.

However, some authors may choose longer launch windows depending on their circumstances. A **three-day, five-day, or week-long launch** can be effective when aligned with available time, energy, and budget. Longer launches may allow for staggered outreach, paid promotion, or expanded platform coverage—but they also require sustained attention and coordination.

The key consideration is capacity. A shorter launch executed well is far more effective than a longer launch that cannot be supported consistently.

Launch length should be a strategic decision, not an assumption. The goal is to match your launch structure to your resources so that momentum is maintained rather than diluted.

Intentional Timing Creates Stronger Results

A launch works best when timing, duration, and coordination are decided in advance. When authors choose a launch date and window intentionally, promotion becomes clearer, more focused, and easier to execute.

The success of a launch is not determined by how long it lasts, but by how well it's supported.

Why Launch Timing Is Often Overlooked

Many authors underestimate how much launch timing affects outcomes. In coaching and book audits, launch timing is frequently an afterthought—despite its measurable impact on visibility and sales.

A launch is not just about what you say, but when you say it. Treating timing as a strategic decision rather than a convenience increases the likelihood that your efforts will translate into meaningful results.

An effective launch doesn't require perfection. It requires intention.

Action Steps: Planning Your Book Launch

1. **Separate Your Publish Date and Launch Window:** Choose a **publish date** (when your book goes live) and a **launch window** (when you actively promote it). Keep your launch within 30 days of publication to remain eligible for "Top New Release" as well as "Best Seller" visibility. Allow enough time between the two for setup, testing, early reviews, and any paid promotion.

2. **Choose Your Launch Timing Strategically:** Schedule your launch during the workweek—midweek is often the most effective. Avoid weekends and major holidays unless your book directly aligns with them.

3. **Review the Calendar for Conflicts:** Check for holidays, major events, and seasonal distractions that could compete for attention. Adjust your timing to work *with* reader behavior, not against it.

4. **Define Your Launch Window:** Decide how long your launch will run (2 days, 3 days, or up to a week). Match the length to your available time, energy, and ability to stay consistent.

5. **Confirm Your Availability:** Make sure you can be fully present during your launch window. Block off time to engage, respond, and actively promote without distractions.

6. **Prepare Your Marketing Assets in Advance:** Everything should be ready before your launch begins. Create and finalize email announcements, social media posts, graphics and visuals, purchase links.

7. **Coordinate Your Promotion Across Platforms:** Decide where you will promote (email, social media, etc.). Align your messaging so all platforms support the same goal at the same time.

8. **Validate Your Book Setup:** Before launching, confirm your book is properly indexed on retailer platforms, displaying accurate metadata, fully functional (links, categories, pricing).

9. **Document Your Final Launch Plan:** Write down publish date, launch dates and window, promotion platforms. Treat this as a commitment—not a placeholder.

10. **Commit to Intentional Timing:** Make your decisions based on strategy, not convenience. A focused, well-supported launch will consistently outperform a rushed one.

Start with a plan, then execute with focus. Strong launches aren't built on urgency—they're built on preparation and timing.

Chapter Three

Building a Launch Team Without Bribery or Begging

Before we talk about building a launch team, we need to reframe what that phrase usually means.

I don't run a traditional launch team. There's no standing group of volunteers, no hype squad, and no expectation that anyone else will carry the weight of my book's success.

Most of the time, **I am the launch team.**

That mindset matters. When you assume full responsibility for your launch, you plan differently.

You prepare more carefully.

You stop hoping people will "come through" and start building systems that work even when they don't.

Any outside support I receive is supplemental. Helpful, yes—but never essential.

That distinction is what turns book launches from emotional rollercoasters into repeatable business processes.

What a Launch Team Actually Does (and What They Don't)

At its core, a launch team exists to provide **early social proof**.

That's the real function—not enthusiasm, not volume, and certainly not blind praise. Social proof tells retailers, algorithms, and potential readers that a book is being engaged with by real people.

This usually shows up as:

- A small number of early reviews

- Initial ratings that establish credibility

- Modest but authentic sharing or discussion

What a launch team does *not* do is create demand out of thin air. It doesn't not guarantee sales, long-term visibility, or success. Those outcomes depend on factors you control: the quality of the book, the clarity of its positioning, and the preparation behind the launch.

Reviews, in particular, deserve a realistic explanation.

They are a necessary evil in publishing. If you plan to hire promoters, most will require a minimum of five reviews and a rating close to five stars before they'll even consider working with you. After launch, reviews continue to matter because Amazon's algorithm factors them into discoverability. More reviews generally increase the likelihood of your book appearing in searches and recommendations.

However, **only honest reviews work over time.**

I'm very clear when I ask for reviews: write what you genuinely think. Flattering but dishonest reviews may temporarily inflate a rating, but they don't build trust—and they can backfire. Readers can sense when feedback feels manufactured.

Negative reviews are uncomfortable, but they're also useful. They highlight mismatches between reader expectations and delivery. If you pay attention, they often reveal where clarity, structure, or positioning can improve. Professionals treat this feedback as information, not as a personal attack.

Where to Find Readers Willing to Help (Even If You're Unknown)

You don't need a formal team or a large platform to get early support. You need access to people who already trust your work in some capacity.

That might include:

- Newsletter subscribers who consistently open or reply

- Readers who comment thoughtfully on your content

- Beta readers or critique partners

- Past clients or colleagues familiar with your expertise

These are not random numbers on a follower count. They are people who have already demonstrated engagement. That matters far more than reach.

I don't make public announcements asking for help. I approach this the way I approach any professional request—selectively and privately. A clear, respectful invitation sets the tone:

"I'm preparing to launch a new book and I'm looking for a few early readers willing to leave an honest review. There's no obligation if timing doesn't work for you."

This framing does two important things. First, it removes pressure. Second, it filters for people who actually want to participate. Reluctant support is rarely effective.

For first-time authors, this approach is especially important. Early relationships set the tone for your publishing career. Protect them. A small group of thoughtful readers will do more for your book than a large group of disengaged ones.

How to Motivate Support Without Money or Guilt

I don't motivate people with incentives, rewards, or emotional appeals.

Instead, I manage expectations the same way I would in a professional environment: through clarity, structure, and respect.

That starts with being specific about what matters.

Reviews are most helpful during launch week. That's when they have the greatest impact on visibility. Sharing the book is optional, not required. Participation is voluntary, and timing may vary.

I also plan for non-participation.

Some people will agree and never follow through. Others will intend to help and miss the window.

This isn't a failure of character—it's a reality of human behavior. I design my launches assuming partial follow-through so I'm never dependent on any single person.

Finally, appreciation is expressed simply. A direct thank-you is enough. Over-the-top praise often signals unspoken expectations, and I avoid that entirely.

When you remove guilt from the process, the people who participate do so because they want to. That's the only kind of support worth building around.

How to Secure Early Readers and Reviews (Without a Formal Launch Team)

This process is intentionally simple. Complexity creates friction, and friction kills follow-through. Your goal is not to assemble a large group—it's to secure *enough* early engagement to support visibility.

Step 1: Identify 10-25 Potential Early Readers

You are not looking for enthusiasm. You are looking for reliability.

Create a short list of people who:

- Have already engaged with your work

- Understand your subject or genre

- Have previously followed through on small requests

This might include newsletter subscribers who reply to emails, past clients, beta readers, or colleagues familiar with your expertise.

Resist the urge to invite everyone. A focused list increases response quality and reduces disappointment.

Step 2: Send a Clear, Low-Pressure Invitation

Reach out privately. One-on-one messages outperform announcements because they feel respectful and specific. Your message should include:

- What the book is

- What you're asking for (early reading and an honest review)

- When reviews are most helpful (basically give them a deadline to submit their review)

- Explicit permission to decline

For example:

"I'm preparing to launch a new book and I'm inviting a small group of early readers to help by leaving an honest review prior/during launch week. If timing doesn't work, no worries at all—I completely understand."

This language does two things: it clarifies the request and removes obligation. Both are essential.

Step 3: Track Commitments Simply

You don't need complicated software.

A basic spreadsheet or document is enough to track:

- Who you invited

- Who accepted

- Who received the book

- Who followed through

This is not about pressure—it's about visibility. Knowing where things stand helps you plan realistically.

Step 4: Provide Clear Instructions at the Right Time

Once someone agrees, tell them exactly what to expect next:

- When they will receive the book

- Where they can leave a review

- When reviews help the most

Avoid sending everything at once. Information overload leads to inaction. One clear message per step is enough.

Step 5: Send One Professional Reminder

A single reminder during launch week is appropriate. More than that becomes pressure.

Keep it brief and neutral:

"Just a quick reminder that reviews this week are especially helpful. Thank you again for supporting this launch."

If someone doesn't respond, let it go. Your system should never rely on chasing individuals.

Step 6: Close the Loop with Appreciation

After launch week, thank everyone who participated.

No guilt. No commentary on who didn't. No emotional framing.

A simple message acknowledging their time and support reinforces goodwill and keeps relationships intact for future projects.

Why This Approach Works

This approach treats early readers as collaborators, not resources. It respects their time, protects your professionalism, and keeps you firmly in control of the launch process.

Most importantly, it scales. You can repeat this exact system for every book—adjusting only the size of your list as your audience grows.

That consistency is what turns launches from stressful events into predictable business operations.

Managing Expectations and Avoiding Launch-Day Chaos

My early book launches felt chaotic because I lacked experience. Instructions weren't centralized. Timelines were unclear. I reacted instead of planning.

That changed when I stopped treating launches as emotional milestones and started treating them as systems.

Now, I can usually predict how a launch will perform before it happens. The predictor isn't luck or enthusiasm—it's preparation. When I'm organized going in, the launch runs smoothly. When I'm not, the results reflect that.

To avoid chaos:

- Set timelines early and communicate them clearly

- Keep all information in one place

- Plan for variability instead of perfection

Most importantly, remember this: **you are the launch manager**.

Any help you receive supports your strategy—it does not replace it.

When you operate from that position, launches become calmer, more professional, and repeatable. You stop chasing validation and start building processes that improve with each book.

That's how sustainable publishing is built—not through begging, not through bribery, but through clarity, preparation, and experience.

Action Steps: Building a Reliable Launch Team

1. **Adopt the "You Are the Launch Team" Mindset:** Start by taking full ownership of your launch. Any support you receive is a bonus—not something you depend on. This shift immediately reduces stress and improves preparation.

2. **Identify 10-25 Reliable Early Readers:** Create a focused list of people who have already engaged with your work and tend to follow through. Prioritize reliability over reach.

3. **Send Personal, Low-Pressure Invitations:** Reach out individually with a clear, respectful message. Explain what you're asking (early reading + honest review), when it matters, and give them permission to decline.

4. **Be Clear About Expectations From the Start**: Let readers know: When they'll receive the book, when reviews are most helpful (launch week or before), and that honesty matters more than positivity. Clarity increases follow-through.

5. **Track Responses Simply:** Use a basic document or spreadsheet to track who you invited, who accepted, and who completed their review. Stay organized without overcomplicating the process.

6. **Send the Book With Clear Next Steps:** When someone agrees, provide simple, step-by-step instructions. Avoid overwhelming them—keep communication focused and timely.

7. **Send One Reminder During Launch Week (or Just Before):** Follow up once with a brief, professional reminder. Don't chase or pressure. Your system should work without constant follow-up.

8. **Plan for Partial Participation:** Assume that not everyone will follow through—and build your plan accordingly. This keeps you from relying too heavily on any one person.

9. **Accept All Feedback Without Interference:** Encourage honest reviews and resist the urge to control outcomes. Even critical feedback provides useful insight and builds credibility.

10. **Thank Participants and Close the Loop:** After launch, send a simple thank-you to those who participated. No guilt, no pressure—just appreciation. This preserves relationships for future launches.

A strong launch team isn't built on hype—it's built on clarity and trust.

When you remove pressure and focus on systems, you create support that's reliable, repeatable, and professional.

Chapter Four

Reviews, Reviews, Reviews (Without Breaking the Rules)

If there is one marketing tool that can make or break a book launch, it's reviews. While advertising budgets, social media campaigns, and email lists all play important roles, nothing carries more weight in the eyes of potential readers than honest, thoughtful feedback from other readers. Yet, the power of reviews comes with a caveat: mishandle them, and you could risk your book being delisted or, in extreme cases, losing your Amazon account entirely.

This chapter is designed to guide you through the process of obtaining reviews ethically and strategically, ensuring that your marketing efforts build credibility without crossing any dangerous lines.

By the end, you will understand why reviews matter more than ratings, how to set up your own Advanced Reader Copy (ARC) team, and the specific pitfalls to avoid if you want to keep you author account in good standing.

Why Reviews Matter More Than Ratings

At first glance, star ratings seem to be the ultimate measure of a book's success. A five-star rating looks impressive, while lower ratings might scare off potential buyers. However, ratings alone tell only part of the story.

Reviews provide context, nuance, and a voice that resonates with readers in a way a number never can. A well-written three- or four-star review that explains why a reader connected—or didn't connect—with your book can influence buying decisions more than silent five-star ratings. It reassures readers that your book is authentic and worth considering, while also helping algorithms recognize engagement.

Amazon's systems favor books that show evidence of meaningful interaction, which makes reviews critical not only for social proof but also for discoverability. In short, ratings grab attention, but reviews hold it.

How to Ethically Gather Early Reviews

Early reviews are essential for establishing momentum, yet the line between "encouraging feedback" and "manipulation" is thin. Amazon explicitly forbids incentivized reviews, review trading, and asking for positive feedback, and these rules apply even to people you know personally.

For example, sending a free copy to a close friend with a note saying "please leave a five-star review" violates Amazon's guidelines. On the other hand, providing a free copy to a reader or subscriber while clearly stating that their honest review is welcome—and required—is entirely acceptable. Transparency is the key.

When asking for early reviews, it's important to emphasize honesty and independence. Reviewers should feel free to share their true opinions without any pressure or expectation.

A practical approach is to offer a free advance copy in exchange for an honest review, specifying that the review should be posted within a set period, often seven to ten days, to align with your marketing timeline. This method allows you to generate authentic feedback while maintaining the integrity required to protect your account.

Understanding Beta Readers, ARC Teams, and Street Teams

Many authors confuse beta readers, ARC teams, and street teams, yet each serves a distinct purpose.

Beta readers are the first line of feedback and are involved in the manuscript before publication. Their role is purely developmental, offering suggestions on plot, pacing, and character development.

These individuals are not asked to post reviews publicly, and their feedback is meant to help you refine your book.

ARC teams, by contrast, are your ethical engine for early reviews. Members receive the book in advance with the explicit understanding that they will read it, write an honest review, and post it within a specific timeframe.

These reviewers should be at arm's length from you—they should not be immediate family, close friends, or anyone with whom you share finances or household space. Amazon monitors relationships and patterns closely, and even well-intentioned requests from close contacts can trigger warnings or account restrictions.

ARC team members are the safest way to generate reviews without risking compliance violations.

Street teams serve a different purpose altogether. Their role is visibility rather than reviews. They help promote your book launch by sharing announcements, social media posts, and recommendations.

While some may independently leave reviews, this is incidental; their primary function is to amplify awareness, not to provide feedback.

Confusing these roles can leave to poorly executed campaigns and, potentially, compliance problems if reviewers feel pressured.

Building a Review Team That Works

Creating an effective review team requires clarity, communication, and careful selection. Begin by inviting readers who are genuinely interested in your book and have a history of thoughtful engagement. This can include email subscribers, past readers, or members of online groups who have shown interest in your genre. Avoid inviting friends, family members, or coworkers, as their reviews could be considered biased and place your account at risk.

Once you have identified potential ARC members, send a clear and professional invitation that explains exactly what you are asking. A well-crafted invitation accomplishes several things: it communicates that participation is optional, it sets expectations for timing and honesty, and it frames the review as a valuable contribution rather than a favor.

To make this concrete, here is an example of an ARC invitation email you could use or adapt:

Sample ARC Invitation Email

Subject: Join My Advanced Reader Team for [Book Title]

Hello [Name],

I'm reaching out because I'm preparing to launch my new book, [Book Title], and I would love for you to be part of my Advanced Reader Team. As a member of this team, you will receive an advance copy of the book before its official release. Your role is simple: read the book and share your honest thoughts in a review on Amazon (and optionally on Goodreads).

Here's what to expect if you join:

1. You will receive a copy of the book in the next few days.

2. Reviews should be posted within 7-10 days after receiving your copy.

3. Reviews should be honest, reflecting your genuine experience. Positive or negative feedback is welcome.

4. Receiving a free copy does not obligate you to leave a positive review.

If this sounds like something you'd like to participate in, please reply to this email to confirm your spot. Space is limited, and I want to make sure everyone who joins can manage the timeline comfortably.

Thank you so much for considering being part of my launch team—I truly value your time and feedback!

Warmly,

[Your Name]

Providing Reviewer Guidelines

To ensure your ARC team succeeds without any confusion, it's helpful to provide a simple one-page guideline. This reinforces expectations, protects your account, and ensures that reviews appear as naturally as possible.

Here's an example of what such a guideline could include:

ARC Reviewer Guidelines

Thank you for joining my Advanced Reader Team! Here's what I need from you:

1. **Read the book fully.** Take notes if you'd like, but reading in full is essential for an honest review.

2. **Write an honest review.** Share what you genuinely liked and any areas where you struggled.

3. **Post your review on Amazon (and optionally Goodreads).** Please include your disclosure that you received an advance copy.

4. **Timeline:** Reviews should be posted within 7-10 days of receiving the book.

5. **Honesty over positivity:** Your experience matters more than a perfect rating. Do not feel pressured to give a 5-star review.

6. **Privacy and transparency:** Avoid copying other reviews, sharing drafts, or discussing your review online before posting.

By following these guidelines, you help ensure that the reviews are compliant, credible, and impactful.

Using Review Platforms Safely

If your personal list of potential reviewers is small, review platforms can supplement your efforts. Tools like Pubby, BookBounty, and Booksprout offer affordable ways to connect with readers willing to provide feedback.

However, these platforms must be used with caution. Do not post review requests in bulk, do not coach reviewers on what to say, and avoid relying exclusively on one service. Repetition, sudden review spikes, and overly similar review language can trigger Amazon's monitoring systems and raise red flags. Platforms are meant to supplement organic ARC efforts, not replace them.

What Not to Do If You Value your Amazon Account

Amazon's policies on reviews are strict, and violations can have serious consequences. Avoid asking friends or family to review your book, exchanging reviews with other authors, offering compensation, or requesting only positive feedback.

Do not try to coordinate reviews across multiple accounts or locations. Even small missteps, such as sending identical review requests to multiple recipients or having multiple reviews posted in rapid succession, can appear suspicious to Amazon's automated monitoring systems. The safest path is transparency, patience, and adherence to clear guidelines.

Final Thoughts

Reviews are not just a marketing tactic—they are a reflection of trust between you and your readers.

When handled ethically, reviews increase credibility, visibility, and engagement. When handled carelessly, they can jeopardize your book and your career.

By creating an ARC team, providing clear instructions and timelines, and respecting Amazon's rules, you can generate early, meaningful reviews that support your launch without risking compliance.

Remember, a thoughtful, well-managed ARC program will always outperform shortcuts.

Treat your reviewers with respect, provide clear guidance, and keep transparency at the center of your approach. Your long-term success as an author depends on it.

Action Steps: Get Reviews Ethically and Effectively

1. **Understand the Rules Before You Start:** Review Amazon's guidelines on reviews so you know exactly what is allowed. Never ask for positive reviews, offer incentives, or use friends and family. Protect your account first and foremost.

2. **Identify Potential ARC Readers:** Make a list of readers who are genuinely interested in your book—email subscribers, past readers, or engaged followers in your niche. Focus on quality and reliability over quantity.

3. **Invite Your ARC Team Professionally:** Send a clear invitation explaining what they'll receive and what's expected. Emphasize that reviews must be honest, not positive. Set a simple deadline (typically 7-10 days.)

4. **Provide Clear Reviewer Guidelines:** Create a short, easy-to-follow document outlining expectations: read the full book, write an honest review, include a disclosure, and post within the timeline. Clarity prevents confusion.

5. **Deliver Advance Copies Early:** Send your book to ARC readers before launch with enough time for them to read and review. Give them a smooth experience—no last-minute scrambling.

6. **Separate Your Teams Clearly:** Keep your roles distinct. ***Beta readers*** = feedback before publishing. ***ARC team*** = honest reviews. ***Street team*** = promotion and visibility. Mixing these roles leads to poor results and potential compliance issues.

7. **Use Review Platforms Carefully (If Needed):** If you need additional reviewers, use platforms like Booksprout or Pubby cautiously. Avoid bulk requests or unnatural spikes in reviews. These tools should support—not replace—your ARC team.

8. **Monitor Review Activity During Launch:** Watch for incoming reviews, but don't panic if they come in gradually. Natural pacing looks more authentic than a sudden surge.

9. **Never Interfere With Reviews:** Do not attempt to edit, influence, or respond defensively to reviews. Let them stand as they are. Authenticity builds trust—even when feedback isn't perfect.

10. **Thank Your Reviewers (Privately, Not Publicly):** Show appreciation to your ARC team through email or direct messages, but never in a way that could be seen as influencing future reviews.

Reviews are built on trust.

Play the long game, follow the rules, and focus on honesty—because one compliant credible review is worth more than ten that put your account at risk.

PART II – Launch Day Strategy

(Make the Most of Your 24-48 Hours)

Chapter Five

What to Do on Launch Day—Hour by Hour

Launch day is not the day to verify, test, or fix your book. It's the day your marketing plan goes live. Authors who treat launch day as a final preparation stage often find themselves dealing with preventable issues under unnecessary pressure.

This chapter is designed to help you approach launch day as a controlled, professional marketing event. By the time launch day arrives, your systems should already be in motion. Your job is to monitor, engage, and document—not troubleshoot major technical problems.

24-48 Hours Before Launch: Verification, Testing, and Automation

The most important work related to launch day happens before launch day begins. At least 24-48 hours prior to your scheduled launch, you should complete all verification and testing tasks. This buffer is critical because publishing platforms, particularly Amazon, do not resolve issues instantly.

If your manuscript, book cover, description, pricing, or categories require correction, platforms may take hours or days to approve changes. In some cases, fixing on issue requires reuploading files, which can temporarily remove your book from sale or reset certain data.

Attempting to address these problems on launch day itself can significantly disrupt your campaign.

During this pre-launch window, you should confirm that your book appears correctly on all platforms where it will be sold. Carefully review formatting, check for display issues on both desktop and mobile, and confirm that your "Look Inside" or preview features function properly. You should also personally test the purchase process to ensure there are no errors or unexpected delays.

Equally important is link verification. Every link you plan to use—whether in emails, social posts, or advertisements—should be tested and saved in a central location. Broken or incorrect links on launch day can cost you sales during the most time-sensitive period of your campaign.

This is also the time to finalize and schedule your promotional messaging. Emails to your list should be written, proofread, and scheduled in advance. Social media posts should be queued using scheduling tools whenever possible. Automation allows your launch to continue smoothly even if you're dealing with engagement, technical questions, or simply managing your own energy.

By the time launch day arrives, you should not be writing posts, drafting emails, or scrambling to locate links. Those decisions should already be made.

Launch Day Morning: Monitoring, Not Fixing

On launch day itself, your role is not to fix systems—it's to confirm that the systems you built are running as expected.

Begin the day by checking your scheduled emails have been delivered and that your automated posts are publishing correctly. Verify that your book is still live and available across platforms, but avoid making unnecessary changes unless a clear problem arises.

At this stage, you should be able to focus on engagement rather than logistics. Respond to messages, acknowledge readers, and monitor early sales activity without falling into constant refreshing or panic-driven checking. The groundwork you laid in the previous 48-hours allows you to stay composed and professional.

Coordinating Emails, Social Posts, and Announcements

Effective launch-day communication is coordinated, not scattered. Your audience will encounter your message in multiple places, and that's expected.

Repetition across channels increases visibility and recall, especially given how algorithms and inbox filtering limit what people actually see.

Your email list remains one of your most important launch assets. Email allows for direct communication and typically converts more reliably than social media. Social platforms, while still useful for awareness and credibility, are increasingly unpredictable when it comes to direct sales.

The effectiveness of any platform depends on your book's topic and where your ideal readers already spend their time. There is no universal formula.

Authors should be cautious about over-investing in social media while neglecting other promotional avenues, particularly those they control, such as email lists or strategic partnerships.

Launch day messaging should feel consistent across platforms while allowing for slight variations in tone and emphasis. Each message reinforces the same core idea: the book is available, and it solves a specific or fulfills a specific need.

Frequency and Professional Visibility

Many authors worry that they're promoting too often. In reality, most authors promote too little.

On launch day, multiple mentions are not only acceptable but necessary. Visibility is created through repetition, especially during a short launch window. As long as your messaging remains clear, respectful, and value-focused, frequent promotion does not damage your credibility.

It's important to remember that not everyone sees every post or email. Strategic repetition ensures that your message reaches different segments of your audience at different times.

Midday: Engagement, Tracking, and Documentation

As sales activity increases on launch day, your responsibility expands beyond promotion and engagement. You must also document your results in real time.

Bestseller rankings and category placements can shift rapidly, and retail platforms do not preserve a historical record of peak positions in a way that is easily accessible later. If you don't capture the moment, it may be gone.

I learned this lesson firsthand during one of my own launches. Sales were strong from the beginning. Based on the value of purchases, it was clear the book should have reached number one in multiple categories.

However, Amazon's ranking system failed to update throughout the most critical period of the launch. The site simply did not reflect what was happening in real time.

I stayed up that entire night refreshing the page, expecting the rankings to adjust and display the bestseller placements I knew had been earned. They did not.

The following day—the final day of the launch—the system finally updated. By that point, the rankings reflected only the current moment, not the peak performance from the day before.

The book did reach number one in one category, which I was able to document, but the additional category placements that had likely occurred during the first day were never visible. There was no way to retroactively capture them.

The sales happened. The momentum was real. But without screenshots taken at the moment of peak ranking, there was no official confirmation for those additional categories. And bestseller status, even for well-known authors, is often temporary. Rankings can rise and fall within hours.

This experience underscores an important principle: monitor your rankings throughout launch day and capture evidence as milestones occur. Screenshots serve as social proof, marketing assets, and professional documentation. Do not assume the data will still be there later. If your book reaches a significant placement, record it immediately.

Handling Technical Issues with Perspective

No matter how well you prepare, technical issues can still arise. A retailer pages may temporarily disappear. A ranking may not update. A link my break. A formatting glitch may appear in the preview. These issues are frustrating, especially on a day you have worked toward for months.

However, the way you respond to technical issues is often more important than the issue itself.

First, pause before reacting publicly. Your initial emotional response should not become your public response. Verify the problem from multiple devices or browsers. Confirm whether it is isolated or platform-wide. Sometimes what appears to be a major issue is a temporary display lag or a caching problem.

Second, have backup systems in place. This is why preparing alternative links ahead of time is critical (if applicable). If on retailer page is malfunctioning, you can direct readers to another.

If your direct link is not working, you can temporarily direct readers to your main author page or website.

If necessary, post a brief, professional message such as:

"There appears to be a temporary issue with the retailer page. We're monitoring the situation. In the meantime, you can access the book here: [alternate link, if possible]. Thank you for your patience."

Clear, composed communication builds trust. Panic-driven messaging erodes it.

It's also important to understand that most readers are far more patient than authors assume. They don't expect perfection from digital platforms. What they expect is professionalism. A technical hiccup does not invalidate your launch unless you allow it to consume your time, energy, and attention for the rest of the day.

Your focus should remain on promotion, engagement, and documentation. If an issue cannot be resolved immediately, escalate it through proper support channels and move forward with the aspects of your launch that are within your control.

Professional authors anticipate friction. They do not allow it to define the outcome.

Choosing Dependable Launch Support

Launch teams, ARC readers, and beta readers are often presented as essential components of a successful book launch. While they can be extremely valuable, their effectiveness depends entirely on who you choose.

Many authors make the mistake of prioritizing quantity over quality. They assemble large teams without evaluating reliability. The result is often inconsistent follow-through, delayed reviews, vague feedback, or commentary that is unrelated to the book's objectives.

A smaller, dependable group is far more powerful than a large, disengaged one.

When selecting beta readers, prioritize individuals who understand your target audience and respect your timeline. Their feedback should be specific, actionable, and aligned with the purpose of your book. General opinions, personal preference that contradict your audience's needs, or excessive nitpicking can derail momentum and create unnecessary doubt close to launch.

ARC readers should be chosen based on their ability to follow instructions and submit reviews on time. Before inviting someone into this role, consider their past behavior. Do they consistently follow through on commitments? Do they communicate clearly? Have they demonstrated professionalism?

It's also helpful to set clear expectations from the beginning. Provide deadlines. Explain what type of feedback is most helpful. Clarify whether you are looking for content-level insight, clarity improvements, or final proofreading observations. Ambiguity leads to unhelpful results.

Being selective is not about seeking praise. It's about building a support system that strengthens your launch rather than complicates it. Honest, well-considered feedback from trusted individuals improves your book. Unfocused opinions from unreliable participants delay progress and increase stress during an already demanding process.

Your launch support team should reduce pressure, not add to it.

Closing the Day and Looking Ahead

As launch day comes to a close, resist the urge to immediately shift into analysis mode or emotional judgment. Instead, conclude the day intentionally.

Acknowledge your readers and supporters publicly. Express appreciation to those who purchased, shared, reviewed, or encouraged you.

Gratitude strengthens relationships and reinforces community around your work.

Next, document your results while they are fresh. Record total sales numbers, ranking placements, email open rates, click-through rates, and engagement metrics. Capture screenshots and store them in an organized folder for future marketing use.

These records will become valuable assets when pitching podcasts, media outlets, speaking engagements, or partnerships.

Then, conduct a brief written debrief for yourself. Identify what worked particularly well.

Did a certain email subject line perform strongly? Did a specific platform drive more engagement? Were there time slots where activity spiked?

Equally important, identify what could be improved next time.

Was there confusion about links? Did you wait too long to communicate a reminder?

Launch day is not the conclusion of your marketing strategy. It's the beginning of your book's lifecycle in the marketplace.

The systems you build—your email infrastructure, automation, documentation process, and support team—are long-term assets.

The insights you gather will shape your approach to future launches, promotional campaigns, and product releases.

Professional authors treat launch day as both an event and a data collection opportunity. The momentum you create does not end at midnight. It transitions into sustained marketing, partnerships, and continued visibility.

The most successful self-published authors understand this principle clearly: launch day opens the door. What you build afterward determines how long it stays open.

Action Steps: Execute a Controlled, Professional Launch Day

1. **Complete All Testing 24-48 Hours Before Launch:** Confirm your book is live, formatted correctly, and purchasable across all devices. Test every link you plan to use. Fix issues early—launch day is not for troubleshooting.

2. **Schedule Your Emails and Content in Advance:** Write, proofread, and schedule your launch emails and social media posts ahead of time. Remove last-minute decision-making so you can stay focused on execution and engagement.

3. **Prepare a Central "Launch Hub" Document:** Keep all your links, messaging, backup links, and key information in one place. This prevents scrambling and allows you to respond quickly if needed.

4. **Start Launch Day by Monitoring, Not Changing:** Check that emails were delivered, posts are publishing, and your book is live. Avoid making unnecessary edits unless there's a clear issue.

5. **Promote Consistently Throughout the Day:** Plan multiple touchpoints across email and social platforms. Vary the angle of your message, but keep the core focus clear: your book is available and valuable.

6. **Engage With Readers in Real Time:** Respond to comments, messages, and replies. Acknowledge support and build momentum through interaction, not just broadcasting.

7. **Track Rankings and Capture Screenshots:** Monitor your rankings and category positions throughout the day. Take screenshots immediately when milestones happen—don't assume the data will still be there later.

8. **Stay Calm if Technical Issues Arise:** Pause before reacting. Verify the issue, use backup links if needed, and communicate clearly and professionally. Keep your focus on what you can control.

9. **Document Key Metrics Before the Day Ends:** Record sales, rankings, email performance, and engagement data. Save screenshots and organize them for future use in marketing and partnerships.

10. **Close the Day With Gratitude and Reflection:** Thank your readers and supporters publicly. Then write a quick debrief: what worked, what didn't, and what you'll improve next time.

Launch day is execution, not experimentation.

Preparation creates control. Control creates confidence. And confidence allows you to show up like a professional when it matters most.

Chapter Six

Tracking Rankings, Sales, and Visibility

Once your book goes live, your focus shifts from preparation to performance.

Launch day is not just about celebration. It's about observation. Rankings move. Categories shift. Sales accumulate. Visibility expands—or stalls.

Tracking rankings, sales, and visibility is not about obsessing over numbers. It's about understanding how Amazon responds to your strategy and using that information to refine future launches.

When you understand what the numbers actually mean, you gain control over your process instead of reacting emotionally to fluctuations.

Understanding Amazon Rankings (And What They Mean)

Amazon's Best Sellers Rank (BSR) reflects recent sales velocity. It does not measure lifetime sales, writing quality, or long-term success. It measures how quickly copies are selling relative to other books in that format.

Because rankings are weighted toward recent activity, they fluctuate—sometimes dramatically.

A concentrated surge in sales during launch can cause a sharp ranking spike. A pause in sales can cause a noticeable drop. This is normal. Rankings are responsive to momentum.

During one of my early launches, I experienced a dramatic spike in rankings. That result was not accidental. It was the outcome of choosing the right keywords and categories and hiring the right promoters to create a concentrated burst of visibility. That coordinated effort created what I describe as a "perfect storm." Out of ten launches (so far) using this structured approach, eight have resulted in #1 Bestseller status.

That point is not to boast. It's to demonstrate that rankings respond to intentional strategy. Categories, keywords, and promotional timing matter. When these elements align, the algorithm responds. Promotional volume also plays a decisive role; reducing exposure during launch almost always produces measurable ranking consequences.

However, the reverse is also true. Rankings can change quickly in the other direction. Early in my publishing career, I did not fully understand how rapidly rankings could move. I missed capturing screenshots when one of my books reached #1 bestseller status. By the time I returned to check, the ranking had shifted and another book had taken my book's place.

I have not made the mistake again.

Rankings are fluid. If you're aiming for a category win, you must be present enough during your launch to capture the moment when it happens.

Category Rankings vs. Overall Store Ranking

Your book receives an overall Amazon ranking and individual rankings within each category where it appears.

The overall ranking compares your book to every other book in that format across Amazon. It's highly competitive and requires significant sales volume to move meaningfully.

Category rankings compare your book only to others within that specific genre or subcategory. These are strategically important.

Before launch, you should know:

- Every category your book is placed in

- The current ranking of the #1 bestseller in each category

- The relative competitiveness of those categories

- How far your book would need to climb to reach a top position

The day before every launch, I create a tracking spreadsheet. I record my book's overall ranking, category rankings, and total copies sold before the launch begins. This provides a clear baseline.

I also document every category the book is currently listed in so I can monitor growth in each one throughout the launch.

One the morning of launch—before promoters begin sending traffic, typically between 9:00 and 10:00 a.m.—I open that spreadsheet and record:

- My book's overall ranking

- My book's ranking in each category

- The ranking of the #1 bestseller in every category my book is in

- Total copies sold as of that morning

This data allows me to measure performance accurately at the end of the launch. I can see exactly how far the book moved, how competitive each category was, and how effectively promotions converted into ranking growth.

Tracking category positions in real time turns launch day into measurable performance analysis instead of guesswork.

	A	B	C	D	E	F
1			Stats from Book Launch, Day 1 and Day 2			
2	Author:		Veronica Goldspiel			
3	Book Title:		Ready, Set, Publish			
4	Dates:		RELEASED: 12/25/2025			
5						
6	Date/Time		Best Sellers List - Day 1	My Sales Ranking	Current #1 Sales Ranking	Downloads
7	1/23/2026	5:00 p.m.	#1 BEST SELLER in Authorship (Kindle Store)	1,201	1,201	152
8			#1 BEST SELLER in Editing Writing Reference (Kindle Store)	1,201	1,201	
9			#2 BEST SELLER in Publishing & Books (Kindle Store)		856	
10			#2 BEST SELLER in Writing, Research & Publishing Guides (Kindle Store)		856	
11			#3 BEST SELLER in Editing Writing Reference (Books)		856	
12			#5 BEST SELLER in Editing Guides (Kindle Store) - CA			
13			#9 BEST SELLER in Authorship (Kindle) - CA			
14			#9 BEST SELLER in Reference eBooks			
15			#25 BEST SELLER in Editing Guides (Books) - CA			
16			#38 BEST SELLER in Writing Reference (Books)			
17						
18			#1 NEW RELEASE in Reference eBooks			
19			#1 NEW RELEASE in Editing Writing Reference (Kindle Store)			
20			#1 NEW RELEASE in Authorship (Kindle)			
21			#1 NEW RELEASE in Publishing & Books (Kindle Store)			
22			#1 NEW RELEASE in Editing Writing Reference (Books)			
23			#1 NEW RELEASE in Writing, Research & Publishing Guides (Kindle Store)			
24			#1 NEW RELEASE in Authorship (Kindle Store) - CA			
25			#1 NEW RELEASE in Writing Guides (Kindle Store) - CA			
26			#1 NEW RELEASE in Writing, Research & Publishing (Kindle Store) - CA			
27			#1 NEW RELEASE in Book Publishing (Kindle Store) - CA			
28			#2 NEW RELEASE in Editing Guides (Books) - CA			
29			#3 NEW RELEASE in Writing Guides (Books) - CA			
30			#4 NEW RELEASE in Writing, Research & Publishing (Books)			
31			#4 NEW RELEASE in Writing, Research and Publishing (Books) - CA			

Example of My Launch Day Spreadsheet

Free Tools and Manual Tracking Methods

You do not need paid software to track your launch effectively. Manual tracking is often more precise and more educational.

A simple spreadsheet is sufficient. What matters is consistency.

Throughout launch day, check rankings regularly.

Historically, Amazon updated rankings approximately every hour. That's no longer consistently the case.

Now, rankings may update only once or twice during an entire day, and the timing is erratic.

Updates are algorithm-driven and triggered by internal factors that are not publicly disclosed.

Because of this unpredictability, consistent monitoring is essential.

If you know your book has sold a significant number of copies and rankings have not updated by late afternoon, you may try to contact Amazon support.

Politely explain that you are conducting a book launch and would like to ensure rankings are reflecting current sales, especially if you are approaching #1 bestseller status and hope to capture screenshots.

Be professional. Be respectful. Sometimes rankings update shortly after such a conversation. Sometimes they do not.

Either way, maintaining professionalism matters. Launch day is an opportunity to build momentum—not conflict.

Once rankings begin to move, I begin taking screenshots when the book enters the top 20 bestsellers in a category and continue capturing images as it climbs.

Each screenshot is labeled with the date and the ranking position.

Below are examples of the screenshots I typically take when a book reaches the #1 Best Seller ranking.

I capture these screenshots for every category in which the book achieves this milestone.

Additionally, I sometimes document the book's progress along the way, taking screenshots as it climbs the rankings.

I always record when the book enters the top ten, but I may also capture moments outside the top ten—particularly if the book appears alongside authors I admire or, candidly, if it surpasses someone I'm excited to see in the rankings.

These records provide a clear view of the book's journey and can be a valuable reference for launch days and promotional planning.

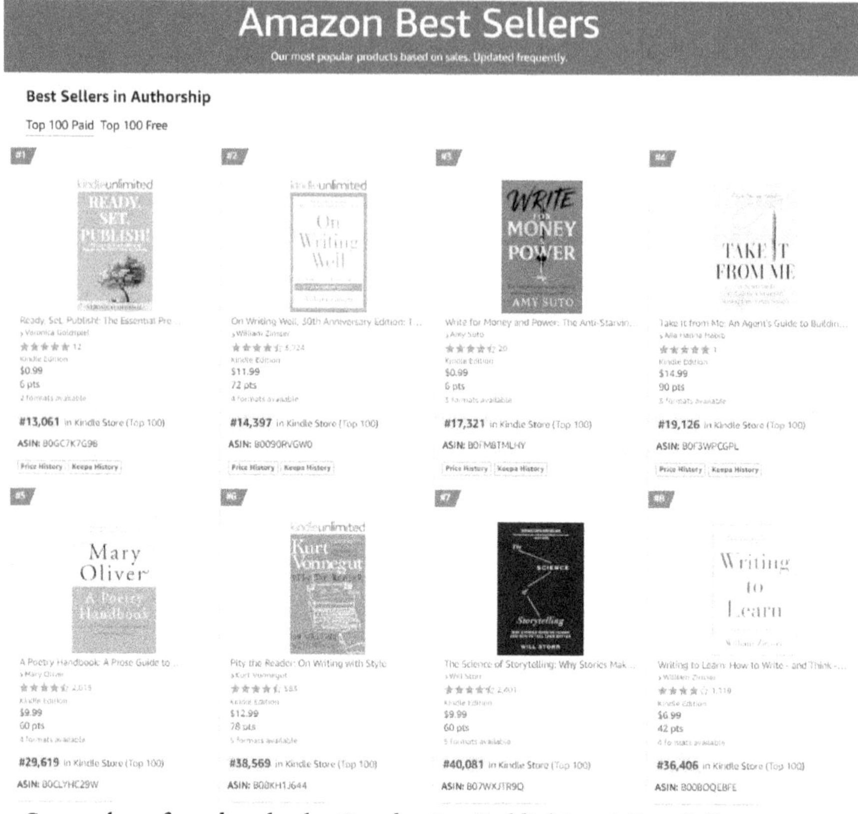

Screenshot of my last book - Ready, Set, Publish! - #1 Best Seller status in Authorship category

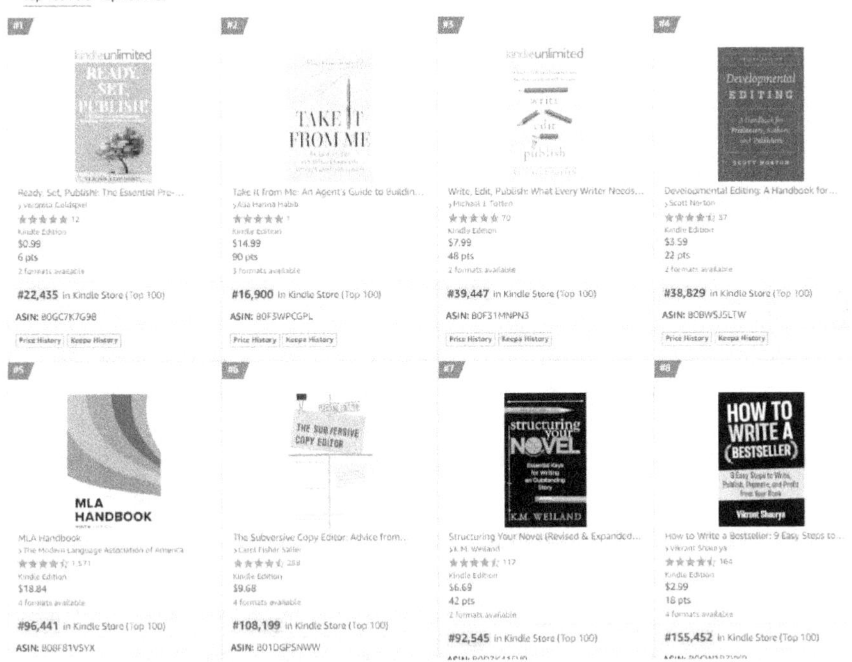

Screenshot of my last book - Ready, Set, Publish! - #1 Best Seller status in Editing Writing Reference category

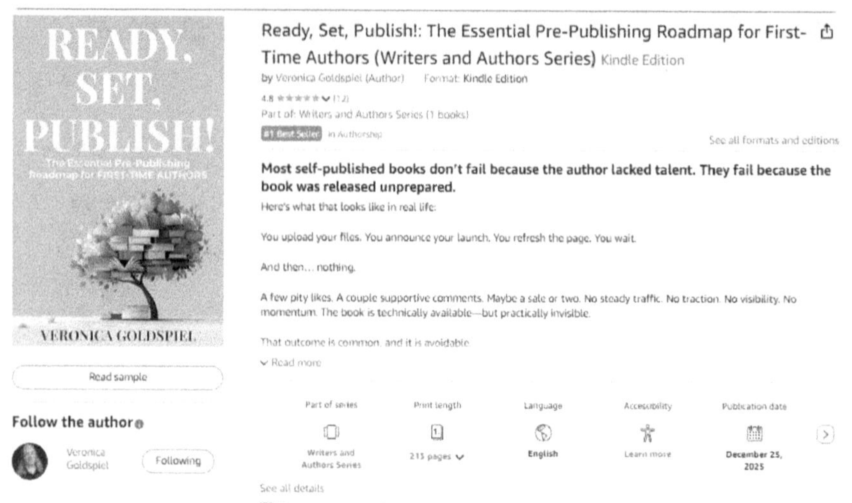

Screenshot of the orange #1 Best Seller status in Authorship

I also make it a point to capture screenshots of the coveted orange flag that appears next to a book's listing when it reaches #1 Best Seller (as seen above), as well as the #1 Top New Release status (as seen below).

I do this for every category in which the book achieves these milestones.

Screenshot of my book, Ready, Set, Publish, at #1 on the New Release category

This documentation is not vanity. It's marketing proof. Bestseller screenshots can be used in media kits, on websites, in email campaigns, and in future promotions.

The day before launch, I also confirm that all social media posts are scheduled and that promoters are aligned.

Launch day should be reserved for monitoring performance, recording data, and capturing milestones—not scrambling to prepare materials.

Clearing your schedule allows you to stay present for ranking movement and capture key milestones as they happen.

When to Celebrate—and When Not to Panic

It's important to interpret ranking movement correctly and to understand what it tells you about your launch's performance.

Celebrate the wins when you reach predefined category goals, secure a bestseller badge, notice sustained upward momentum, or see your book enter stronger "Customers Also Bought" ecosystems.

These are all signs that the algorithm is responding and that your promotional efforts are effective.

At the same time, don't panic when rankings drop after a spike, updates are delayed, or sales activity slows once a promotional window ends.

Temporary declines are simply a reflection of how Amazon calculates recent sales velocity. They do not erase the success of your launch. Maintaining perspective is key.

The most important step in preparing for launch is defining success before it begins.

Determine in advance what ranking constitutes a win, which categories you are targeting, and what actions you will take if movement stalls.

Clear benchmarks allow you to measure outcomes objectively rather than emotionally.

I learned this lesson firsthand during one launch that didn't perform as expected. I had reduced the number of promoters I hired compared to previous campaigns, assuming the impact would be minimal.

That book became one of only two in my career that did not reach #1 bestseller status. The data was clear: less promotional force resulted in less ranking movement.

For the next launch, I committed to hiring a minimum of three promoters per day throughout the launch window. That book reached #1 bestseller status, and every subsequent book following that approach achieved at least one #1 category ranking.

The lesson was straightforward: consistency in promotional volume directly influences ranking outcomes. Tracking patterns allows you to make informed adjustments, and those adjustments create repeatable success.

Launch week is not a mystery—it is a measurable event.

By approaching rankings, categories, promoters, and documentation with structure and discipline, you transform launch day from an emotional rollercoaster into strategic execution.

After multiple launches, I no longer see ranking movement as highs and lows. Instead, I view it as feedback.

Every spike, delay, and category shift provides insight into visibility, promotional strength, and positioning.

When approached with preparation, data, and discipline, rankings stop feeling unpredictable and become actionable indicators that give you confidence.

One practical way to celebrate and document your success is by creating a Best Seller collage. When your book reaches #1 Best Seller and/or #1 Top New Release status, compile screenshots from all categories where the book achieved these milestones.

These collages are perfect for sharing with readers, thanking your promotional partners, and highlighting your achievement on social media.

The collage also serves as a visual record of your launch's success, showing not only the outcome but the journey your book took to reach those milestones.

Best Seller collage for my book, Ready, Set, Publish!

Track carefully. Promote strategically. Stay present. When you build structure around your launch, the results will reflect the discipline and preparation you put into them.

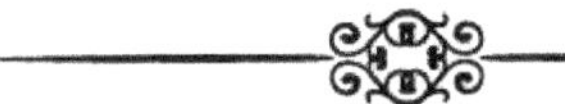

Action Plan: Track Rankings, Sales, and Visibility with Strategies (Not Stress)

1. **Establish Your Baseline Before Launch:** The day before your launch, record your starting point: overall ranking, category rankings, and total copies sold. This gives you a clear "before" snapshot so you can measure real progress instead of guessing.

2. **Map Your Categories and Competition:** List every category your book appears in and identify the current #1 book in each. Not their rankings so you understand what you're up against—and what it will take to climb.

3. **Create a Simple Tracking System:** Set up a spreadsheet to log key data: rankings (overall + category), sales, and time of check-ins. Keep it clean and consistent—this is your launch-day command center.

4. **Monitor Rankings Throughout Launch Day:** Check your rankings periodically during launch. Not obsessively refreshing every second—but consistently enough to catch meaningful movement.

5. **Record Key Milestones in Real Time:** As your book climbs, documents when it enters the top 20, top 10, and hits #1 in any category. These moments matter—and they can disappear fast if you're not paying attention.

6. **Capture Screenshots as Proof:** Take clear screenshots of rankings, especially when you hit #1 Best Seller or Top New Release. Label them with dates and categories so you can actually use them later (future-you will be grateful).

7. **Prepare to Stay Present on Launch Day:** Schedule promotions, emails, and posts in advance so your only job on launch day is tracking performance and capturing wins—not scrambling.

8. **Define Success Before You Launch:** Decide in advance what counts as a win: a specific category rank, hitting top 10, or achieving a bestseller badge. This keeps you grounded when rankings inevitably fluctuate.

9. **Analyze What the Data Is Telling You:** After launch, review your numbers. Which promotions drove movement? Which categories responded fastest? Where did momentum stall? This is how you turn one launch into a repeatable system.

10. **Use Your Results as Marketing Assets:** Turn your screenshots into social proof—collages, website graphics, email highlights. Your rankings aren't just numbers; they're credibility you can reuse again and again.

Build Clarity, Not Chaos

Tracking is not about fixating on numbers—it is about understanding how the system responds to your actions. When you approach your launch with a data-driven mindset, you replace uncertainty with insight and position yourself to make informed, strategic improvements over time.

Chapter Seven

Categories, Keywords, and Discoverability Strategy

Discoverability on Amazon is not a matter of luck—it is a result of deliberate positioning. Every author wants visibility, ranking momentum, and, ideally, bestseller status. Yet many underestimate just how much these outcomes depend on decisions made before a single copy is sold.

Categories and keywords are far from mere administrative details; they are strategic tools that quietly shape placement, competition level, search visibility, and ranking potential.

Over the course of publishing multiple books and securing repeated #1 bestseller rankings, I've learned that discoverability must be engineered—it does not happen by accident. This chapter will guide you through how to do it effectively.

Why Categories Are Silent Salespeople

When you publish through Amazon KDP, one of the first decisions you make is selecting your book's categories. Most authors treat this as a formality, but it is anything but.

Categories determine where your book is positioned within Amazon's ecosystem, which bestseller lists you are eligible for, the level of competition you are entering, and ultimately how realistic your ranking goals are.

Each category operates as its own competitive arena. A broad category may require hundreds of daily sales to reach #1, while a more targeted subcategory could require far fewer. That difference matters.

In every launch, my goal is to create the strongest possible environment for success. This means choosing categories based not only on topic alignment but also on competitive analysis.

I learned this the hard way during a launch where Amazon reassigned my book to a category that did not match my strategy or launch criteria. The result was an environment that did not support my goals.

Once I corrected the category in my KDP dashboard, I observed a noticeable improvement in the book's ranking. The lesson is clear: categories are not static labels—they are strategic placements that require attention and maintenance.

Choosing Smart, Competitive Categories

My approach to category selection is intentional and data-driven. The first step is identifying logical category paths based on your book's core topic. I start by reviewing Amazon's category tree, examining books similar to mine and noting where they are positioned.

Relevance is essential; your book must genuinely fit the category, as misalignment can harm credibility and reader trust.

Next, I study the top 10 books in each subcategory. I examine their Best Sellers Rank (BSR), review count, price point, and positioning. This helps me assess the sales velocity required to compete.

While Amazon does not disclose exact sales numbers, experienced publishers know that a lower BSR corresponds to higher sales volume.

For example, a category where the #1 book has a BSR of 4,000 is more competitive than one where the top book has a BSR of 40,000. The goal is not to find the easiest category but one that provides a realistic opportunity given your launch strategy.

Finally, I confirm category competitiveness immediately before launch, typically the day prior.

Markets shift and sales velocity changes, so a category that looked promising weeks earlier may have become significantly more competitive. By verifying before launch, you ensure that your book is strategically positioned rather than leaving its success to chance.

Using Keywords for Organic Discovery

If categories determine where your book competes, keywords determine whether it is found. Amazon allows seven backend keyword fields, and I use all seven for every book.

Early in my publishing journey, I underestimated keyword research. For two of my first ten books, I selected what I believed were "good" keywords without data or analysis, and those launches underperformed.

Once I mastered keyword research, ever subsequent book reached #1 bestseller status, with some even achieving #1 International Bestseller recognition.

Effective keywords are directly related to your book's topic, based on actual search behavior, and structured as search phrases rather than single words.

For instance, "Mindset" is a weak keyword, whereas "Mindset for female entrepreneurs" reflects buyer intent and aligns with how readers search.

My research process includes observing Amazon's search bar autofill, analyzing high-ranking competitors, identifying problem-based phrases readers use when seeking solutions, and validating search demand with tools such as Publisher Rocket.

Each keyword box allows up to 50 characters, so it's important to use full phrases and avoid repeating your title or selecting overly generic terms. Most importantly, your keywords should align with your categories to create a consistent positioning story.

Updating Categories After Launch

Many authors assume that once a book is live, nothing can be changed. This is not true. Markets evolve, competition shifts, and reader behavior changes.

Periodically reviewing your category placement—every 60-90 days or whenever visibility declines—is a smart practice. If a category becomes saturated or misaligned, you can update it through your KDP dashboard or contact support.

Strategic repositioning can restore visibility and improve ranking potential. Discoverability is not a one-time setup; it requires ongoing maintenance.

International Visibility and Momentum

Strong category positioning and keyword alignment in your primary market can extend visibility into international marketplaces.

Two of my books reached #1 International Bestseller status without additional category adjustments abroad. The results were driven by disciplined strategy executed well in the primary market, showing that solid positioning can amplify reach across territories.

International rankings are rarely accidental—they are usually a byproduct of strong launch strategy and execution.

The Strategic Difference

The difference between my early underperforming launches and later consistent bestseller launches was precision, not talent. Casual category selection and guesswork with keywords yielded inconsistent results.

Once I committed to research, confirmation, alignment, and optimization, outcomes improved significantly. While no category or keyword can guarantee a bestseller ranking, strategic placement substantially increases the probability of success.

Think of discoverability as infrastructure: it creates visibility, and visibility creates opportunity.

Action Steps: Track and Improve Your Book's Visibility During Launch

1. **Audit Your Current Categories:** Review the categories your book is listed in and make sure they accurately reflect your content while still offering a realistic chance to rank. Aim for balance between relevance and opportunity.

2. **Study the Top 10 Books in Each Category:** Look at the leading books in your chosen categories. Pay attention to their Best Sellers Rank (BSR), positioning, and overall competitiveness. This gives you a clear picture of what you're up against.

3. **Upgrade Your Backend Keywords:** Replace broad, single-word keywords with specific, search-driven phrases your ideal reader would actually type in. Think in terms of intent, not just topics.

4. **Recheck Category Competitiveness Before Launch:** Categories can shift quickly. The day before your launch, review your selected categories again to ensure they still give you the best chance of visibility and ranking.

5. **Monitor Rankings During Launch Week:** Track your book's performance daily (or hourly) during launch. Watch how your rankings move and note what activities (emails, posts, promotions) impact visibility.

6. **Adjust Based on Real Data:** If your book isn't gaining traction, don't guess—adjust. Test new categories or refine keywords based on what you're seeing in real time.

7. **Schedule a 60-Day Discoverability Review:** Set a reminder to revisit your categories, keywords, and rankings every 60 days. Visibility is not a one-time setup—it requires ongoing refinement.

Positioning for a Concentrated Launch Window

My launch strategy is short and concentrated, typically two days, with the eBook priced at $0.99 to maximize conversion velocity.

After the launch window, the price increases to standard, while the paperback remains at full price throughout. Because the launch is brief, category and keyword optimization must be completed well before the first promotional email is sent.

During launch, momentum is driven by curated promoters, email lists, strategic partnerships, social visibility, and external traffic. Advertising is a post-launch amplification tool, not a replacement for strong initial discoverability.

In this concentrated structure, sales velocity directly drives ranking movement. Poorly chosen categories or misaligned keywords at this stage can compromise discoverability when it matters most.

Preparation, verification, and strategic execution before launch are critical—because the window may be short, but the effort behind it is anything but.

PART III – Organic & Low-cost Promotion Strategies That Work

Chapter Eight

Selling Books Without Amazon Ads or Facebook Ads

Many authors believe that paid advertising is required to sell books. It's an easy assumption to make—ads promise visibility, reach, and quick results.

However, advertising is not a substitute for strategy. It is a tool designed to amplify what is already working. Without a strong foundation in place, ads tend to magnify weaknesses, often leading to wasted time, money, and energy without producing lasting results.

This chapter focuses on how to sell books organically, why this approach often leads to stronger long-term conversions, and how to prepare your book for paid amplification only after you've built the right infrastructure.

The Long Game vs. Quick Spikes

It's relatively easy to create temporary spikes in sales. These often come from short-term tactics like heavy launch discounts, paid ad campaigns, coordinated promotions, or intense launch-day exposure.

While these spikes can create the appearance of success, they rarely translate into sustained visibility. Once the promotion ends, sales often return to their previous levels, leaving authors wondering what went wrong.

Long-term growth, on the other hand, comes from building systems that continue working long after launch week is over. At the core of this approach are a few key elements: audience ownership, authority positioning, optimized discoverability, and relationship-building.

Owning your audience—primarily through an email list—allows you to communicate directly with readers regardless of algorithm changes. Establishing authority in your niche builds trust, making readers more likely to purchase.

Optimized categories and keywords ensure your book appears in front of readers actively searching for it. And consistent engagement with your audience and collaborators fosters loyalty and repeat purchases.

Before even considering ads, it's important to evaluate whether your book has this foundation in place. Every element of your listing and marketing should contribute to ongoing visibility, not just a temporary spike.

Why Ads Fail for Most New Authors

Ads are appealing because they seem like a shortcut to visibility, but most authors struggle with them—not because ads don't work, but because the groundwork hasn't been laid. Advertising rewards optimization, testing, and data. Without those elements, it simply amplifies inefficiencies.

One of the most common issues is an unoptimized book listing. Your title, subtitle, cover, and description are the first things a potential reader sees. If these elements are unclear or unconvincing, even high traffic won't convert into sales. Similarly, incorrect or overly broad categories and keywords limit both organic and paid visibility, making it harder for ads to reach the right audience.

Another major factor is the lack of social proof. Reviews play a critical role in building trust, and without them, readers are far less likely to take a chance on a book—no matter how they found it.

Beyond that, many authors lack backend systems such as an email list, which means even when ads do generate interest, there's no way to nurture those readers into long-term supporters.

There's also the issue of expectations. Ads are rarely profitable immediately. They require testing, iteration, and ongoing refinement. Add to that the complexity of advertising platforms—where costs, reach, and performance constantly fluctuate—and it becomes clear why so many authors feel frustrated.

The solution is straightforward: build your infrastructure first. Ads should enhance what's already working, not act as the starting point.

My Position on Facebook Ads

At this stage in my author journey, I don't use Facebook Ads as part of my strategy. I have experience with them from my work as a social media manager, so I understand the mechanics—audience targeting, pixel tracking, creative testing; and performance analysis. However, managing Facebook Ads effectively requires consistent attention, time, and ongoing adjustments to maintain a positive return.

For now, I've chosen to simplify. My focus is on organic systems and, when appropriate, post-launch Amazon Ads. This approach allows me to maintain control without dividing my attention across too many moving parts.

That doesn't mean I've ruled out Facebook Ads entirely. If they align with my goals, resources, and data in the future, I may integrate them. But the key takeaway is this: focus on the channels you can manage well. Simplicity and consistency often outperform trying to do everything at once.

Organic Traffic Sources That Convert

Organic traffic consistently outperforms cold traffic because it comes from readers who already know, like, and trust you. That trust reduces friction and increases the likelihood of conversion.

One of the most powerful tools is an email list. Unlike social platforms, email is an owned channel, meaning no algorithm can limit your reach. Readers who join your list have already expressed interest, making them far more likely to engage with your content and purchase your book.

Building an email list typically starts with a reader magnet—a free resource aligned with your book's topic—promoted across your platforms. Over time, nurturing that list with valuable, consistent communication creates a reliable source of conversions for every launch.

Podcast interviews are another highly effective channel. When you appear on a podcast, you benefit from the trust the host has already built with their audience. This borrowed credibility introduces you to listeners who are already primed to engage.

With a thoughtful pitch, clear talking points, and strong follow-up, podcast appearances can generate visibility, authority, and sales without requiring financial investment.

Social media, when used strategically, also plays a key role. Rather than focusing solely on selling, the most effective approach is to create content that educates, entertains, or inspires—while naturally tying back to your book's message. Consistency is what builds familiarity, and familiarity builds trust. Over time, that trust translates into sales.

In-person opportunities, such as book fairs, signings, or speaking engagements, add another dimension. Face-to-face interaction builds a level of connection that digital methods often cannot replicate. These experiences not only lead to immediate sales but also foster long-term reader relationships and word-of-mouth promotion.

Finally, partnerships and collaborations can significantly expand your reach. By working with authors, influencers, or organizations in your niche, you gain access to audiences that already trust the person introducing you. When approached strategically, these collaborations can generate highly qualified traffic without any ad spend.

Promotion Strategies That Cost Time, Not Money

Even without a marketing budget, meaningful promotion is absolutely possible. It simply requires a willingness to invest time and effort instead of money.

Creating a reader magnet is one of the most effective starting points. This could be a checklist, guide, short story, or any resource that complements your book and encourages readers to join your email list. Guest opportunities—such as podcasts, blogs, or niche publications—allow you to share your expertise while naturally introducing your book to new audiences.

Content creation also plays a major role. Whether through blog posts, social media, or video, consistently producing valuable content establishes authority and keeps you visible. While these efforts may not produce instant results, they build durable marketing assets that continue working across multiple book launches.

Ads as Amplifiers, Not Foundations

Once your organic systems are in place and functioning well, advertising can become a powerful scaling tool. At that stage, ads help extend your reach, maintain ranking momentum, and reinforce visibility. However, their effectiveness depends entirely on the strength of the foundation beneath them.

Successful advertising requires testing, monitoring, and data-driven adjustments. When used correctly, it amplifies proven conversions and improves return on investment. When used too early, it often leads to frustration and wasted resources. Timing matters.

Adaptability Is The Real Skill

The self-publishing landscape is constantly evolving. Platforms change, algorithms shift, and reader behavior adapts over time.

Success doesn't come from rigidly following a single strategy—it comes from observing, adjusting, and staying flexible.

Organic infrastructure provides stability in this ever-changing environment.

Your email list, authority, and optimized listings act as a foundation that remains steady even when external factors shift.

Advertising, when layered on top of that foundation, can accelerate growth—but it should never replace it.

Action Plan: Sell More Books Without Relying on Ads

1. Audit Your Book Listing for Discoverability: Review your title, subtitle, keywords, categories, and book description. Make sure they are clear, specific, and aligned with what your ideal reader is actually searching for. Small improvements here can significantly increase visibility.

2. Strengthen Your Book Description: Rewrite or refine your description so it focuses on reader outcomes, not just content. Make it easy to scan, emotionally engaging, and clearly answer: *Why should someone read this?*

3. Create (or Improve) Your Lead Magnet: Develop a simple, high-value resource that connects directly to your book. This gives interested readers a reason to join your email list and stay in your ecosystem beyond a single purchase.

4. Start Building Your Email List Immediately: Add your opt-in link inside your book, on your website, and across your platforms. Focus on consistent growth—even a few subscribers per week compounds over time.

5. Commit to a Weekly Content Rhythm: Choose a platform and begin posting consistently. Share insights, lessons, stories, and ideas related to your book. Focus on providing value rather than trying to "sell" in every post.

6. Identify 3-5 Guest Opportunities: Look for podcasts, blogs, newsletter, or communities where your ideal readers already exist. Pitch yourself with a clear angle that provides value to their audience, not just promotion for your book.

7. Explore One Strategic Partnership: Find another author, creator, or brand with a similar audience and collaborate. This could be cross-promotion, a joint event, or shared content. Partnerships expand your reach faster than working alone.

8. Consider One Offline Opportunity (If Relevant): Look for local events, workshops, book signings, or speaking opportunities that align with your topic or genre. In-person connection can build strong reader relationships quickly.

9. Track What's Working (and Do More of It): Pay attention to where your sales, engagement, or subscribers are coming from. Double down on the strategies that produce results instead of constantly chasing new ones.

10. Add Paid Ads Only After This Is Working: Once you have consistent visibility, a growing audience, and a clear message, then consider ads. At that point, you'll be scaling something proven—not guessing.

Build the foundation first.

Organic strategies create stability, trust, and long-term growth. Ads don't fix a weak system—they amplify a strong one.

Do You Need Support?

If you'd like support reviewing your own setup, I offer a Deep Dive Book Audit where I evaluate your Amazon listing, Author Central page, and even your book's interior experience (with permission). The goal is to identify what may be limiting your discoverability or conversions and provide clear, prioritized recommendations so you know exactly what to adjust and improve.

You can learn more here: https://goldspielcreativeenterprises.com/deep -dive-book-audit/

Chapter Nine

Social Media That Actually Sells Books

Many authors approach social media from one of two extremes. Some believe it will magically generate book sales with minimal effort, while others dismiss it entirely as a noisy distraction that leads nowhere.

In reality, neither view is accurate. Social media is not a shortcut to instant success, but it is far from useless.

When used intentionally, it becomes a long-term system that steadily builds visibility, trust, and ultimately, sales.

This chapter will help you approach social media with clarity instead of confusion.

You'll learn how to choose the right platform without spreading yourself thin, what to share when you don't feel like "selling," how to create content that naturally leads readers toward your book, and how to talk about your work consistently without feeling repetitive or uncomfortable.

Social media can absolutely sell books—but only when it's approached with purpose.

Choose the Right Platform Instead of All of Them

One of the most common mistakes self-published authors make is trying to be everywhere at once.

It's easy to feel like you *should* be on every platform—Instagram, TikTok, Facebook, LinkedIn, Pinterest, YouTube, Threads, X—but that approach often leads to burnout rather than results.

Each platform operates differently. They attract different audiences, favor different types of content, and reward different behaviors.

Success doesn't come from being present everywhere; it comes from being effective somewhere.

The key is alignment. Ask yourself where your ideal reader already spends their time. Consider what type of content feels natural for you to create consistently.

A nonfiction author targeting professionals may feel more at home on LinkedIn, where thoughtful insights and industry knowledge perform well.

A romance author might thrive on visually driven or emotionally engaging platforms like Instagram or TikTok.

A children's author may find strong opportunities in Pinterest or Facebook communities centered around parents.

Instead of trying to manage multiple platforms poorly, focus on one primary platform and one secondary platform.

This allows you to go deeper—learning what works, understanding your audience, and building real relationships. Over time, this depth creates far more impact than shallow visibility across many channels.

The right platform amplifies your effort. The wrong one drains it.

What to Post When You Don't Want to "Sell"

Many authors hesitate to show up on social media because they associate posting with self-promotion. They don't want to feel pushy, repetitive, or overly sales-focused—and that hesitation often leads to inconsistency or silence.

The solution is not to avoid talking about your book, but to reframe how you think about it.

You are not simply promoting a product. You are offering something valuable—whether that's knowledge, entertainment, emotional connection, or transformation. If your book helps, inspires, or resonates with readers, then sharing it is not self-serving. It's useful.

When you don't feel like "selling," shift your focus to value-driven content.

This might mean teaching a small concept from your book, sharing a behind-the-scenes moment from your writing process, or posting an excerpt that sparks curiosity. You could offer a practical tip related to your topic or ask a thoughtful question that invites engagement.

Content like this builds trust over time. It shows your audience what you know, how you think, and what they can expect from your work.

Instead of telling people to buy your book, you demonstrate why it matters. And when readers consistently gain something from your content—whether that's insight, inspiration, or clarity—they naturally become more interested in going deeper through your book.

Content Ideas That Quietly Lead to Sales

The most effective content rarely feels like advertising. Instead, it feels relevant, helpful, or engaging. When your content connects with your audience in a meaningful way, sales become a byproduct rather than the focus.

Problem-Solution Content

One powerful approach is problem-solution content. Identify a specific challenge your ideal reader faces and offer a clear, concise solution. This immediately positions you as helpful while naturally connecting your expertise to your book. A simple mention that you explore the topic further in your book is often enough.

Sharing Transformation Stories

Another effective strategy is sharing transformation stories. These can be personal or drawn from your experiences, but they should highlight change—a clear "before and after." Readers are drawn to growth and authenticity, and when they understand why you wrote your book, they're more likely to feel connected to it.

Challenge Common Misconceptions

You can also create posts that challenge common misconceptions in your niche. By addressing and correcting these myths, you position yourself as a credible voice while reinforcing the value of your perspective.

Reader-Focused Content

Similarly, reader-focused content shifts attention away from what your book *is* and toward what it *does*. Instead of listing features, focus on outcomes—what readers will understand, feel, or be able to do after reading.

Create Short Educational Series

Another strong approach is creating short educational series. When you explore a theme over multiple posts, you build anticipation and consistency. Your audience begins to expect and look forward to your content, and by the time you mention your book as a more comprehensive resource, the connection feels natural.

Across all of these approaches, the goal is the same: create content that earns attention by being useful, interesting, or meaningful. Sales follow when that connection is strong.

How to Talk About Your Book More Than Once Without Cringing

Many authors worry that they talk about their book too much.

In reality, most audiences don't see nearly as much of your content as you think. Algorithms limit visibility, followers come and go, and attention is constantly divided. What feels repetitive to you is often brand new to someone else.

The key is not to say less—it's to say it differently.

Instead of repeating the same message, vary your angle. One post might highlight a quote, while another explains a key lesson. You could share a reader review, talk about your motivation for writing the book, or clarify exactly who the book is for—and who it isn't. You can answer common questions, address objections, or expand on specific ideas within the book.

This approach keeps your content fresh while reinforcing the same core message. You're not repeating yourself—you're strengthening recognition through different perspectives.

It's also important to separate your identity from your results. If a post doesn't perform well, it's not a rejection of you or your work. It's simply feedback. Use that data to refine your approach rather than retreat from sharing.

Over time, your book should feel like a natural part of your content—not something you occasionally mention, but something consistently present.

When your audience begins to associate you with your topic and your message, your credibility grows. And as visibility increases, so do sales.

The Long Game

Social media rarely produces immediate results, especially for authors. It works through accumulation—of content, of trust, and of attention.

In the beginning, your posts may receive little engagement. That's normal.

What matters is consistency. Continue showing up, refining your message, and paying attention to what resonates. Over time, small improvements compound into meaningful progress.

Focus on being consistent rather than perfect. Prioritize value over volume, clarity over cleverness, and connection over virality.

These principles may not produce overnight success, but they build something far more reliable: an audience that knows you, trusts you, and wants to support your work.

When approached strategically, social media shifts from feeling like an obligation to becoming a powerful asset. It allows you to reach readers directly, build relationships over time, and create a steady pathway to your book.

Done well, it doesn't just generate likes.

It generates readers.

Action Steps: Turn Social Media Into a Sales Tool

1. **Choose Your Primary Platform (And Commit to It):** Pick one platform where your ideal readers are most active and where your content style feels natural. Then choose one secondary platform if you have the capacity. Ignore the rest for now—focus creates results.

2. **Define Your Content Pillars:** Identify 3-4 types of content you will consistently create, such as *educational content* where you teach something from your book, *personal content* where you share your journey or writing process, *engaging content* like questions, opinions, or discussions, and *promotional content* that highlights your book, reviews, or offers. This gives your content structure and prevents you from guessing what to post.

3. **Create 10 Simple Post Ideas Before You Start:** Remove daily pressure by brainstorming ahead. Use ideas like a lesson from your book, a short excerpt, a common mistake in your niche, a reader-focused outcome, or a personal story tied to your message. Clarity upfront makes consistency easier.

4. **Post 3 Times This Week (No Overthinking):** Take action immediately. Don't wait for perfect graphics or perfect wording. Focus on showing up. Momentum matters more than perfection at this stage.

5. **Add a Soft Call-to-Action to Every Post:** At the end of your posts, gently guide readers toward the next step. Examples include "I go deeper into this in my book," "This is something I break down in Chapter 3," or "If this helped, you'd love the full book." Keep it natural, not forced.

6. **Talk About Your Book in 5 Different Ways:** Write five posts about your book from different angles, including a quote, a lesson, why you wrote it, who it's for, and a reader result, which helps you get comfortable with repetition through variety.

7. **Engage for 10 Minutes After Posting:** Reply to comments, respond to messages, and interact with others in your niche. Social media rewards interaction—and relationships drive long-term sales.

8. **Track What Gets Attention:** Pay attention to which posts get more engagement, saves, or replies. Don't guess—observe. Then create more content similar to what resonates.

Start where you are. Stay consistent. Adjust as you go.

Social media becomes powerful the moment you stop treating it like a guessing game—and start using it with intention.

Chapter Ten

Email Lists—Your Secret Weapon

I f social media is rented land, your email list is property you own. Platforms change constantly.

Algorithms shift without warning. Accounts can lose reach overnight, or disappear entirely. What feels stable today can become unreliable tomorrow.

An email list, however, operates differently. It gives you a direct, uninterrupted line to readers who have actively chosen to hear from you.

For self-published authors—especially those publishing through Amazon KDP—this is not just helpful, it's essential.

An email list becomes a long-term asset that protects your career, strengthens your book launches, and allows you to build meaningful relationships with readers that extend far beyond a single title.

In this chapter, you'll learn why email consistently outperforms social media, how to build a list from scratch without relying on gimmicks, what to send after your launch is over, and how to turn casual readers into loyal, long-term fans.

Why Email Still Beats Social Media Every Time

Social media is excellent for discovery. It helps new readers find you, encounter your ideas and become aware of your work. But discovery alone does not drive consistent sales. That's where email comes in.

Email is powerful because it creates focused attention. On social media, your content competes with endless distractions—other creators, trending topics, and algorithm-driven feeds. Even your most engaged followers may never see your posts.

With email, your message arrives directly in someone's inbox, where the environment is quieter and the intent is stronger.

There's also a fundamental difference in ownership. Social media audiences are borrowed. Your visibility is controlled by a platform that can change the rules at any time. An email list, on the other hand, is something you build and maintain. It belongs to you.

Perhaps most importantly, the people on your email list have opted in. They've made a conscious decision to hear from you. That level of intent creates a different kind of relationship—one that leads to higher engagement and more consistent purchasing behavior.

When you launch a new book, promote an offer, or invite readers into something deeper, your email list will almost always respond more reliably than social media. If your goal is to build a sustainable author business—not just publish a single book—email isn't optional. It's foundational.

Building a List From Zero (Without Giveaways)

Many authors assume they need complicated funnels, paid ads, or elaborate contests to grow an email list.

In reality, growth starts with something much simpler: clarity. When your offer is clear and relevant, the right readers will respond.

Lead Magnets

One of the most effective—and often overlooked—strategies is placing a dedicated lead magnet page inside your book. This page should appear both near the beginning (after the introduction) and again at the end. Instead of directing readers to your social media, invite them to receive something specific and valuable.

This could be a bonus chapter, a companion workbook, a checklist, a resource guide, access to a private reader community, or even a short video training related to your topic.

The key is alignment. Whatever you offer should naturally extend the promise of your book, making it feel like a continuation rather than a separate promotion.

Your message should be simple and benefit-focused. Readers should immediately understand what they'll gain and how to access it. A clear, easy-to-type link matters more than clever wording.

And timing matters too—readers who have just engaged with your book are already interested and more likely to subscribe.

Live Experiences

Another powerful way to grow your list is through live experiences. Hosting a free workshop, masterclass, or short challenge creates a natural reason for people to join your list. These events position you as an authority while attracting readers who are genuinely interested in your topic.

For nonfiction authors, this might look like a focused training session, a multi-day implementation challenge, or a live Q&A.

Fiction authors can take a different angle—offering behind-the-scenes writing sessions, character deep-dives, or themed events connecting to their genre.

In every case, registration requires an email address, which turns interest into a tangible connection.

Calls-To-Action

Beyond these strategies, consistent calls-to-action play a critical role. People won't join your list unless you regularly invite them to. That invitation should appear across your ecosystem—on your website, in your social media bio, in pinned posts, in video descriptions, and inside every book you publish.

The language you use matters. Instead of asking people to "join your newsletter," focus on what they'll receive. When the benefit is clear—whether it's a guide, a toolkit, or exclusive content—conversions increase naturally.

You can also offer content upgrades tied to specific pieces of content you create. If you publish a blog post, video, or educational resource, provide an additional downloadable asset that helps readers go deeper. Those who want more will opt in.

You don't need a large audience to start building a list. You need a relevant offer, clear positioning, and consistent visibility.

What to Email Your List After Launch

A common mistake authors make is treating their email list as a one-time tool for launch week. They build it, promote heavily during release, and then go quiet. When that happens, the relationship fades quickly.

Your list should not only hear from you when you want something. It should hear from you because there's ongoing value in staying connected.

After your launch, shift your focus from promotion to relationship-building. If you write nonfiction, continue expanding on ideas from your book.

Share insights that didn't make it into the final manuscript, offer additional examples, or clarify concepts that readers may still be exploring.

If you write fiction, keep the story alive in different ways. Share character backstories, alternate scenes, or insights into your writing process. Give readers a reason to remain emotionally connected to your world.

You can also bring your audience into your journey. Let them see what you're working on next, what inspired your ideas, and what you're learning along the way. This kind of transparency builds trust and makes readers feel invested in your progress.

Another effective approach is highlighting reader feedback. Sharing testimonials, emails, or success stories reinforces the value of your work while reminding subscribers why they joined your list in the first place. It also strengthens the sense of community around your writing.

Occasionally, offer something exclusive. This might include early access to new releases, discount codes, private workshops, beta reader opportunities, or live Q&A sessions. When readers know your email list provides access they can't get elsewhere, its value increases.

Consistency matters more than frequency. Whether you mail once a week or twice a month, what matters is that your audience knows you'll show up regularly with something worth reading.

Turning Casual Readers Into Long-Term Fans

The difference between a one-time reader and a long-term supporter comes down to relationship. An email list gives you the ability to build that relationship intentionally, rather than leaving it to chance.

Start by speaking directly to your readers' needs. When possible, segment your list based on interests or behaviors so your emails feel more relevant. The more aligned your message is with what your readers care about, the more engaged they will be.

At the same time, consistently reinforce your core message. Every email should subtly remind readers who you help, what you help them achieve, and why your perspective matters. This kind of repetition builds familiarity and authority over time.

It's also important to invite interaction. Encourage your subscribers to reply. Ask questions, request feedback, and create opportunities for conversation. When readers respond, the dynamic shifts. Your emails are no longer a broadcast—they become a dialogue. That shift significantly increases loyalty.

Finally, think beyond individual emails and focus on the bigger picture. Your email list should connect to a larger ecosystem that includes your books, events, courses, and any community spaces you create. Each piece should support the others, creating a cohesive experience for your readers.

When people feel seen, supported, and consistently served, they don't just consume your work—they stay connected to it.

Email Is a Long-Term Asset

An email list doesn't grow overnight. It builds gradually through consistent effort, clear offers, and thoughtful placement across your platforms and books.

But once it grows, it becomes one of your most reliable tools. It allows you to launch new work without starting from zero. It gives you access to readers who already know your voice, trust your ideas, and are ready to support what you create next.

That's the real power of email.

It's not just a marketing channel. It's a direct, lasting connection to the people who want more from your work—and are willing to follow you whether you go next.

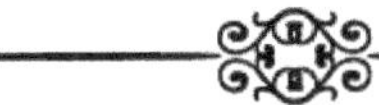

Action Steps: Build and Start Using Your Email List

1. **Choose Your Primary Platform (And Commit to It):** Pick one platform where your ideal readers are most active and where your content style feels natural. Then choose one secondary platform if you have the capacity. Ignore the rest for now—focus creates results.

2. **Define Your Content Pillars:** Identify 3-4 types of content you will consistently create, such as *educational content* where you teach something from your book, *personal content* where you share your journey or writing process, *engaging content* like questions, opinions, or discussions, and *promotional content* that highlights your book, reviews, or offers. This gives your content structure and prevents you from guessing what to post.

3. **Create 10 Simple Post Ideas Before You Start:** Remove daily pressure by brainstorming ahead. Use ideas like a lesson from your book, a short excerpt, a common mistake in your niche, a reader-focused outcome, or a personal story tied to your message. Clarity upfront makes consistency easier.

4. **Post 3 Times This Week (No Overthinking):** Take action immediately. Don't wait for perfect graphics or perfect wording. Focus on showing up. Momentum matters more than perfection at this stage.

5. **Add a Soft Call-to-Action to Every Post:** At the end of your posts, gently guide readers toward the next step. Examples include "I go deeper into this in my book," "This is something I break down in Chapter 3," or "If this helped, you'd love the full book." Keep it natural, not forced.

6. **Talk About Your Book in 5 Different Ways:** Write five posts about your book from different angles, including a quote, a lesson, why you wrote it, who it's for, and a reader result, which helps you get comfortable with repetition through variety.

7. **Engage for 10 Minutes After Posting:** Reply to comments, respond to messages, and interact with others in your niche. Social media rewards interaction—and relationships drive long-term sales.

8. Track What Gets Attention: Pay attention to which posts get more engagement, saves, or replies. Don't guess—observe. Then create more content similar to what resonates.

Start small, but start now!

Your email list doesn't grow because of intention—it grows because of consistent action.

Chapter Eleven

Content Marketing for Authors

Content marketing is one of the most strategic long-term promotional tools available to self-published authors. Unlike temporary marketing tactics, content marketing builds authority, trust, and visibility over time. It positions you not only as a writer, but as a credible voice within your niche or genre. When implemented intentionally, it supports book sales, attracts opportunities, and strengthens your author brand in measurable ways.

Throughout my own publishing journey, I have used consistent blogging and podcasting to promote my expertise, services, and books.

My website blog serves as an educational resource for authors navigating their publishing path, while my podcast, *From Writer to Author: The Podcast*, extends those conversations in a more in-depth and accessible format.

Each time I published aligned content, I see a noticeable increase in website traffic, reader inquiries, and book sales. This correlation reinforces an important principle: when content aligns with your brand and serves your audience well, it drives meaningful engagement.

This chapter explores how blogging, podcasting, and guest posting function as promotional tools; how to write content that naturally leads readers to your books; how to repurpose content strategically; and how to create evergreen assets that support your visibility year-round.

Blogging, Podcasting, and Guest Posting as Promotion

Blogging is one of the most powerful forms of owned media. When you publish articles on your own website, you control the messaging, the audience relationship, and the call to action.

For non-fiction authors, blog posts can address common challenges your readers face, offer practical instruction, or expand on themes explored in your books.

For fiction authors, blogging may involve sharing research, discussing genre themes, exploring character development, or offering insight into the writing process.

The key is relevance. Your blog content should reflect your expertise and reinforce the outcomes your book promises. When readers consistently find value on your website, trust develops. Trust leads to interest, and interest leads to sales.

Podcasting extends this authority into a different medium and a different audience. Through my podcast, *From Writer to Author: The Podcast*, I approach topics that directly affect authors and support their development through their publishing journey.

The spoken format allows for deeper explanation and connection while reinforcing the same brand message presented in my written content. The result is a cohesive ecosystem where blog posts, podcast episodes, services, and books support one another.

In addition to hosting your own platform, appearing as a guest on other podcasts expands your reach significantly. When you speak to an established audience that already trusts the host, your credibility transfers more quickly. I have seen firsthand how guest appearances increase visibility and attract new readers who may not have encountered my work otherwise.

However, effectiveness depends on alignment. The podcasts you appear on must serve the same audience you aim to reach.

Across all formats, the objective is not to promote aggressively It's to demonstrate value. When your expertise is evident, the invitation to explore your book or services feels like a natural next step rather than a sales pitch.

Writing Content That Leads Readers to Your Book

One of the most common mistakes I observe among self-published authors is the lack of alignment between their content and their books or services.

They create blog posts, social media updates, or podcast episodes that may be informative but don't reinforce their broader brand message. As a result, the content generates activity without advancing their goals.

Content must serve a clear purpose. Before creating any piece, ask yourself what outcome you want to achieve. Are you seeking increased visibility, higher book sales, more podcast invitations, greater media coverage, or more clients? Your content strategy should reflect that objective.

Start with the core promise of your book. What transformation or experience does it offer? Every piece of content should relate to that central promise. If your book helps authors move from manuscript to publication, your content should address stages of that journey. If your novel explores resilience or redemption, your content might discuss themes, emotional arcs, or research connected to those ideas.

Content should function as a bridge. It should solve part of the problem while making it clear that a deeper, more comprehensive solution exists within your book. This doesn't require overt selling. Instead, include intentional calls to action that guide readers toward your book page, your email list, or your services.

Alignment creates cohesion. Cohesion builds authority. Authority drives results.

Repurposing Content Across Platforms

Creating consistent content doesn't require constant reinvention. Strategic repurposing allows you to maximize the value of each idea.

A single blog post can become the foundation for a podcast episode. The same episode can be segmented into short-form content for email newsletters or social media. Key teaching points can be adapted into guest articles tailored to external platforms. The message remains consistent, but the format changes to suite the audience and channel.

Repurposing ensures your brand message is reinforced across multiple touchpoints. Readers often need repeated exposure before taking action. When they encounter consistent themes and expertise across platforms, recognition grows.

This strategy also prevents fragmentation. Rather than producing disconnected pieces of content, you build a unified body of work that supports your author identity and long-term objectives.

Evergreen Content That Sells Books Year-Round

While timely topics can generate short bursts of engagement, evergreen content builds lasting visibility. Evergreen content addresses foundational issues, recurring questions, and enduring themes that remain relevant regardless of season or trend.

In my own experience, articles and podcast episodes that address the ongoing challenges authors face continue to generate traffic long after publication. Because the topics are tied to the broader journey of becoming and developing as an author, they remain valuable to new audiences discovering the content for the first time.

For nonfiction authors, evergreen topics often include step-by-step guides, industry fundamentals, mindset challenges, or strategic frameworks.

For fiction authors, evergreen content may explore genre tropes, historical settings, character psychology, or storytelling techniques.

When evergreen content includes a clear pathway to your book or services, it functions as a long-term promotional asset. Over time, a library of aligned, evergreen material can consistently introduce new readers to your work without requiring constant promotional effort.

Action Steps: Build a Content Marketing System That Supports Your Book

1. **Audit Your Existing Content for Alignment:** Review your current content (blog posts, podcasts, guest appearances, social media). Ask: does this clearly support my book's promise and my long-term goals? If not, identify what needs to be adjusted, refined, or removed.

2. **Define Your Primary Objective for the Next 6 Months:** Choose one clear focus: Increase book sales; Grow visibility; or Attract clients or opportunities. Let this objective guide your content topics and calls to action.

3. **Clarify Your Core Content Themes:** Identify 3-5 themes that directly connect to your book. These will become the foundation of your content, ensuring consistency and relevance across platforms.

4. **Create a Quarterly Content Plan:** Map out content for the next 90 days based on your core themes. Focus on quality and consistency—not volume.

5. **Develop Cornerstone Content Pieces:** Create in-depth content that addresses the most important topics in your niche. These pieces should reflect your expertise and directly support your book.

6. **Repurpose Each Piece Strategically:** For every cornerstone piece, create at least three additional formats (posts, emails, short-form content, etc.) This extends reach without requiring constant new ideas.

7. **Include a Clear Call to Action in Every Piece:** Each piece of content should guide the reader to a next step: join your email list, explore your book, engage with your work. Clarity increases conversion.

8. **Build a Library of Evergreen Content:** Focus on content that remains relevant over time. This creates long-term value and reduces the need to constantly produce new material.

9. **Stay Consistent with a Sustainable Schedule:** Choose a publishing rhythm you can maintain (weekly, biweekly, etc.). Consistency builds trust and visibility over time.

10. **Evaluate and Adjust Regularly:** Review your content performance monthly or quarterly. Identify what's working, what's not, and refine your approach accordingly.

Focus on alignment, not volume. When your content consistently supports your book and your goals, it becomes a long-term asset—not just activity.

Chapter Twelve

Goodreads, BookBub, and Reader Platforms

R eader platforms offer significant potential for visibility, credibility, and long-term growth. However, their effectiveness depends entirely on how intentionally they are used.

Many self-published authors create accounts on major reader platforms with high expectations, only to abandon them when immediate results fail to appear. The problem is rarely the platform itself. It's the absence of alignment, clarity, and strategic focus.

Reader platforms should serve your broader publishing objectives. Whether your goal is increased book sales, expanded visibility, or growth in service-based offerings, your activity must reflect that outcome.

When approached strategically, these platforms extend your reach to active readers and engaged communities.

When approached reactively, they become time-consuming obligations with minimal return.

This chapter examines how to use Goodreads effectively, how to approach BookBub organically without relying on a Featured Deal, how reader communities and niche platforms can expand your influence, and how determine what is worth your time.

How to Use Goodreads Without Screaming into the Void

Goodreads is one of the largest reader-centered book discovery platforms available to authors. However, it was designed primarily for readers, not for authors seeking promotion. Understanding this distinction is essential.

Authors who treat Goodreads as a broadcast channel often experience minimal engagement. Readers use the platform to track their reading, write reviews, join discussions, and receive recommendations. They are not there to be marketed to directly.

The foundation of an effective Goodreads presence is a well-optimized author profile. Claim your profile, ensure your biography reflects your positioning and expertise, and include professional imagery and links to your website. Verify that all editions of your books are listed accurately. Reviews and ratings on Goodreads contribute to social proof that influences buying decisions beyond the platform itself.

Although I have not yet experimented with Goodreads Giveaways or group participation, both remain viable strategic options for the coming year. Giveaways can increase book visibility and shelf adds, particularly when aligned with a specific launch or promotional goal. Participation in relevant groups, when approached with a service mindset, can build recognition over time. The key is thoughtful contribution rather than self-promotion.

Goodreads is most effective as a credibility builder and discovery engine. It's a long-term visibility tool rather than a quick sales driver.

Organic BookBub Strategies (No Featured Deal Required)

Bookbub is widely recognized for its competitive Featured Deals, but many authors overlook its broader capabilities as a reader discover platform.

Even without a Featured Deal, claiming and optimizing your BookBub author profile is essential. A clear and professional biography, updated book listings, and consistent branding strengthen your discoverability. Readers can follow authors on BookBub, making follower growth a valuable long-term asset.

Encouraging readers to follow you on BookBub should be part of your ecosystem. Include your follow link in your newsletter, website, and email signature. As your follower count grows, your organic reach increases.

Although I have not yet experimented with BookBub Ads, they remain a strategic option that I will be exploring and testing in the very near future. Unlike Featured Deals, ads allow controlled budgeting and targeting. They can be particularly useful for price promotions or series starters.

Organic success on BookBub depends on consistency and alignment. It's not a one-time promotional event. It's a visibility asset that compounds over time.

Reader Communities and Niche Platforms

While large discovery platforms certainly matter, I have found that niche communities often produce stronger and more meaningful results. My participation in targeted reader and author communities on Facebook has led to increased visibility for my books and services, more direct inquiries, and a noticeable rise in authors reaching out for guidance on their publishing journey.

This experience reinforced an important principle for me: alignment drives engagement. When my ideal audience is already present and actively participating in a community, my contributions generate genuine interaction. Because my expertise directly addresses their needs, conversations naturally turn into relationships. Visibility in the right environment leads to meaningful opportunities.

I approach these communities with a value-first mindset. I offer thoughtful advice, answer questions carefully, and contribute insights without leading with promotion. Over time, members begin to associate my name with expertise and reliability. That recognition creates trust, and trusted leads to organic interest in my books and services without the need for direct selling.

Niche platforms may not always have the largest audiences, but they often provide the highest-quality engagement. For authors who offer services in addition to books, this focused interaction can be especially effective. When you are present in spaces where your ideal readers and clients already gather, your marketing becomes less about broadcasting and more about building relationships.

What's Worth Your Time—And What Isn't

One of the most important marketing decisions I have made in my author business is choosing where not to spend my time. Simply having a presence on a platform does not guarantee visibility. Engagement is what matters. If the right people are not interacting with your content, your effort is not producing meaningful return.

I made the decision to discontinue activity on X and Instagram after recognizing that my ideal audience was not actively engaging with me there. Maintaining a consistent presence required time and energy, yet the results were minimal. Over time, the effort created more frustration than momentum. That realization was not a failure. It was strategic discernment.

Effective marketing requires focus. When I evaluate a platform, I look for measurable indicators: engagement, website traffic, and conversations that lead somewhere productive. If a platform consistently generates interaction and growth, I continue investing in it. If sustained effort produces little return, I reassess and redirect my time.

The objective is not to be visible everywhere. It's to be visible where it matters. Concentrating your efforts on platforms where your audience is already active allows you to build authority efficiently while protecting your writing time and mental energy.

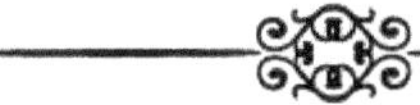

Action Steps: Use Reader Platforms Strategically

1. **Optimize Your Goodreads and BookBub Profiles:** Review both profiles and ensure they are complete, professional, and aligned with your author brand. This includes your bio, author photo, book listings, and links. First impressions matter—treat these profiles as extensions of your book.

2. **Choose One Strategic Experiment:** Identify one focused action to test over the next 6-12 months. Examples: Running a Goodreads Giveaway, participating in a targeted discussion group, increasing engagement through reviews or recommendations. Keep it simple and measurable.

3. **Actively Grow Your BookBub Following:** Encourage readers to follow you on BookBub by adding your follow link to your website, including it in your newsletter, mentioning it occasionally in your content. Track your follower growth and watch for patterns tied to your promotions.

4. **Identify Where You're Already Gaining Traction:** Look at platforms or communities where you've seen engagement. Ask: Where are people responding? What type of content or interaction is working? Use this data to guide your focus.

5. **Analyze What's Driving Engagement:** Go deeper into what's working. Are you answering questions consistently? Sharing useful, specific insights? Participating in the right conversations? Once you identify patterns, repeat them intentionally.

6. **Create a Sustainable Participation Schedule:** Decide how often you will engage on these platforms (e.g., a few times a week). Keep it realistic. Consistency matters more than intensity.

7. **Audit All Platforms You're Using:** Write down every platform where you have a presence. Evaluate each one based on audience alignment,

engagement levels, inquiries or opportunities generated, measurable outcomes.

8. Eliminate or Reduce Low-Performing Platforms: If a platform consistently produces little to no results, reduce your effort or step away entirely. Reallocate that time and energy to platforms that are working.

Focus on alignment and results—not activity. Reader platforms become powerful when you use them intentionally, measure performance, and invest where engagement already exists.

PART IV – Working With Promoters & Outside Help

Chapter Thirteen

Hiring Book Promoters Without Getting Scammed

I f you plan to treat your book like a business asset, then promotion must be approached as a business decision.

I hire promoters for every book I launch. Not randomly. Not emotionally. Strategically. I work from a vetted list of professionals who have proven reliable over time. When used correctly, promoters can strengthen your launch visibility and improve your chances of strong sales momentum. In some cases, that momentum can contribute to bestseller status. However, bestseller results are never guaranteed. Too many variables influence the outcome—competition, timing, pricing, marketing demand, category selection, and audience readiness.

Promotion increases exposure. It does not promise outcomes.

In this chapter, I want you to understand four things in depth:

1. What legitimate book promotion actually looks like.

2. The red flags that should immediately stop you.

3. The questions you must ask before hiring anyone.

4. When hiring promoters makes sense—and when it does not.

What Legitimate Book Promotion Looks Like

Legitimate promotion is structured, transparent, and measurable.

A real book promoter clearly outlines their services. You should see defined offerings such as newsletter features, genre-specific email blasts, promotional placements, advertising management, or coordinated launch packages. Their pricing should be clearly listed or formally quoted. Their process should be explained in plain language.

Professionalism leaves evidence.

A legitimate promoter will typically have:

- A corporate email address tied to their business domain (not Gmail, Hotmail, Yahoo, or other personal accounts).

- A real, functioning website that outlines their services.

- Transparent pricing or clearly defined packages.

- Testimonials from verifiable authors.

- A visible track record within specific genres.

If someone claims to be a business but operates entirely through direct messages and a free email account, that is not a professional infrastructure. Serious businesses invest in their presentation and systems.

In my own launches, I maintain strict cost control. I do not spend more than $60 on any single promoter. Some of the promoters I use charge around $25. Others charge up to $60. For each day of my launch, I typically schedule two to three promoters. This allows me to spread visibility across multiple audiences while keeping my total launch budget manageable.

Instead of placing a large financial bet on one expensive service, I diversify across reputable, affordable platforms. That strategy reduces risk and increases exposure.

Professional promotion should feel organized—not chaotic. You should know what you are paying for, when it will happen, and what audience is being reached.

Read Flags and Promises That Should Make You Walk Away

Now we need to address what should immediately stop you.

The first and most obvious red flag is guarantee. No ethical promoter can guarantee bestseller status, a specific sales number, or national media placement. Anyone making those promises is either manipulating narrow category rankings or using unrealistic claims to secure payment.

The second red flag is unsolicited outreach. Established promoters do not spend their time cold-emailing authors. Authors contact them. If someone approaches you first with an offer, proceed cautiously.

Another warning sign is the use of personal email accounts for business operations. Professional businesses operate through branded domains. A promotional company using a generic email service as its primary contact should be questioned.

You should also be cautious if:

- There is no real website.

- Pricing is hidden or vague.

- Testimonials cannot be verified.

- There is no clear explanation of what the service includes.

- You are pressured to "act today."

I receive many messages that look legitimate at first glance. Polished graphics. Convincing language. Urgent offers. I delete them all. Not because promotion is unnecessary—but because serious professionals do not operate that way.

The most common pattern behind authors getting scammed is simple: they responded to someone who contacted them, and they failed to research thoroughly.

You must reverse that pattern. You initiate contact. You verify credibility. You control the decision.

Questions to Ask Before Hiring Anyone

When you are considering hiring a promoter, you are conducting due diligence. You are not hoping to be chosen. You are evaluating whether they meet your standards.

Ask direct questions.

What audience does your platform reach?

What genres perform best with your service?

How large is your email list or distribution network?

What is your average engagement rate?

What exactly is included in this package?

When will my promotion run?

What do you need from me?

You should also ask for examples of past promotions. A reputable promoter should be able to show previous placements or campaigns.

Clarify payment terms. Understand refund policies. Read the agreement carefully.

In addition, evaluate whether your book fits their audience. Promotion only works when there is alignment. Exposure to the wrong audience is wasted exposure.

The more clarity you demand, the safer your investment becomes.

When Promoters Make Sense—and When They Don't

Hiring promoters makes sense when your foundation is solid.

Your book should be professionally edited. Your cover should be strong. Your description should convert. Your categories should be researched. Your pricing strategy should be intentional. Your audience should be defined.

Promotion amplifies preparation. It does not compensate for its absence.

Hiring promoters also makes sense when you understand your own processes. I consistently advise authors to learn their systems before delegating them. If you do not understand how your launch operates, you cannot properly manage outsourced support.

You cannot delegate your entire author journey. When you attempt to hand over every responsibility, you lose oversight. And once you lose oversight, you risk your reputation.

Everything done in your name reflects on you. Your credibility is an asset. Protect it fiercely.

Hiring promoters does not make sense if you are hoping someone else will "handle everything" while you disengage. It does not make sense if you are unclear on your goals or unwilling to monitor performance.

You remain the decision-maker at all times.

Where to Find Legitimate Book Promoters

Finding reputable promoters requires research.

Start by studying successful authors in your genre. Look at the newsletters where their books are featured. Pay attention to promotional platforms that consistently appear in your category.

Explore reputable book promotion directories and genre-specific email services. Examine websites carefully. Review testimonials. Verify social proof. Look for consistency in branding and messaging.

You can also learn from author communities. Professional writing groups and publishing networks often share experiences and recommendations.

To support you further, I will include a list of the promoters I frequently use in the resources section at the back of this book. These are services I have personally vetted and incorporated into my own launch strategies.

Use that list as a starting point—not as a substitute for your own due diligence.

Action Steps: Hire Book Promoters Without Getting Scammed

1. **Finalize Your Book First:** Before hiring anyone, ensure your book is fully professional with editing completed, cover design polished, and formatting finalized.

2. **Refine Your Book Description:** Write a high-converting description that clearly communicates your book's value and hooks potential readers.

3. **Select Your Categories Strategically:** Research and choose categories that maximize discoverability while aligning with your book's content and audience.

4. **Set Your Launch Pricing Strategy:** Decide on pricing that supports your launch goals—whether that's visibility, sales, or rankings.

5. **Create a Launch Calendar:** Outline each promotional day and activity in advance. Include deadlines for sending materials, posting promotions, and follow-ups.

6. **Determine Your Launch Budget:** Know exactly how much you can spend per day and per promoter. Stick to your budget to avoid overspending.

7. **Identify Reputable Promoters:** Select two to three trusted promoters per launch day, based on experience, reviews, and alignment with your book's genre.

8. **Contact Promoters Directly:** Reach out via their official websites or verified channels. Avoid third-party brokers or unofficial contacts.

9. **Confirm Dates and Secure Placements in Advance:** Lock in your promotional dates and provide all required materials ahead of time to ensure smooth execution.

10. Monitor Results and Document Performance: Track metrics such as traffic, sales, and engagement. Record what worked and what didn't for future launches.

Plan deliberately, invest wisely, and stay actively involved. Remember: promotion should amplify a professional book—not fix it. Your foundation—editing, design, formatting, and positioning—must be in place before you spend a dollar on marketing.

Chapter Fourteen

Book Blogs, Influencers, and Reviews

In the modern publishing landscape, visibility is manufactured through advertising—but credibility is earned through third-party validation. Book blogs, social media influencers, and reader reviews form a powerful ecosystem that shapes purchasing decisions long after launch week fades. Readers trust readers. They trust reviewers who have built consistent voices and communities. And they often trust influencers more than ads.

Your role as an author is not to chase every account with a bookshelf backdrop and a ring light. Your role is to build a strategic, professional reviewer outreach system that creates sustainable visibility.

Let us approach this the way a professional would.

Finding Reviewers Who Actually Review

The first mistake authors make is confusing aesthetics with activity. A beautifully curated Bookstagram page is not necessarily a functioning review platform. Some accounts exist for visuals. Others exist for affiliate links. Others post once every three months and still list "open to review requests" in their bio from years ago.

You are not looking for accounts that look impressive. You're looking for accounts that produce consistent, recent, genre-aligned reviews.

Start with relevance. If you write historical romance, a horror-focused BookTok creator is not your audience—even if they have a large following. Study what they regularly post. Look at the last ten reviews. Do they cover your genre? Do they engage thoughtfully with similar themes or tropes? Would your book naturally fit into their feed without feeling forced?

Then evaluate activity. A reviewer who actually reviews shows patterns. They post consistently—ideally multiple times per month. They engage with their audience in comments. They follow through on announced reading lists. Most importantly, their reviews are recent. If their last full review was five months ago, your email may enter a digital black hole.

Follower count is one of the least useful metrics in this process. A reviewer with 2,500 highly engaged followers who regularly comment and share posts can generate more meaningful attention than an account with 50,000 passive scrollers. Engagement signals influence. Silence signals inflated numbers.

Professional authors track outreach. Create a working document where you log the reviewer's name, platform, genre focus, contact method, date contacted, and response status. Data removes emotion from the process. It also prevents the awkward mistake of pitching the same person twice because you forgot.

If you approach this casually, you will receive casual results. If you approach it methodically, you build leverage.

Outreach Scripts That Don't Get Ignored

Reviewers receive a constant stream of requests. Many are clearly copied and pasted, addressed to the wrong name, or so long they read like back-cover copy plus an autobiography.

Your message must do three things quickly: demonstrate relevance, establish fit, and respect their time.

Begin by showing that you know who they are. Reference a recent review or a specific post. Not in a flattery-heavy way—just enough to signal that you did your homework. A reviewer can tell instantly whether you have read their content or simply scraped their email address.

Next, position your book in reader-focused terms. This is not the moment to describe your writing journey or the years you spent drafting. Instead, articulate the genre, the hook, and the comparable titles or themes. Reviewers think in terms of their audience. Help them see how your book serves that audience.

Keep the pitch concise. Two short paragraphs are usually sufficient. Offer the book in their preferred format and clarify that there is no obligation to leave a positive review. Ethical reviewers value independence. Pressure damages trust.

Tone matters. Professional. Polite. Direct. Avoid desperation and avoid arrogance. You are offering value, not begging for rescue—and not assuming entitlement.

A final strategic note: send your outreach in waves rather than all at once. If every review appears within the same 48 hours, visibility spikes and vanishes. Staggered reviews extend your book's presence across weeks or months. Momentum beats noise.

Managing Rejection Without Spiraling

Rejection is not a possibility in reviewer outreach. It is a certainty.

Some reviewers will not respond. Some will decline politely. Some will say the book is not a good fit. Occasionally, someone may accept the book and never post a review. And yes, sometimes the review itself may be lukewarm.

The difference between amateur and professional authors lies in interpretation.

Amateurs personalize rejection. Professionals analyze it.

If your response rate is low examine your targeting. Are you pitching reviewers who rarely accept indie authors? Are you outside their genre? If multiple reviewers mention pacing or tone concerns, not that for future craft improvement. Feedback—even indirect feedback—is information.

Create emotional distance through numbers. If you send forty outreach emails and receive six acceptances, that is not failure. That is a conversion rate. In many marketing contexts, that is a strong one.

You must also remember that reviewers are not employees. Many operate unpaid, balancing reading with full-time jobs. They are protecting their time and their brand. Respecting a "no" without argument preserves your reputation. Publishing is smaller than it appears.

When rejection triggers doubt, return to process. Refine your list. Improve your pitch. Continue outreach. Momentum cures spiraling.

Using Review Platforms and Paid Review Communities

In addition to direct outreach to bloggers and influencers, there are structured platforms designed to connect authors with readers willing to leave reviews. Services such as BookBounty, BookSprout, and Pubby offer systems that streamline the review acquisition process.

Each platform operates differently. Some focus on distributing Advance Review Copies (ARCs) to readers who opt in based on genre preference.

Others function on credit systems or structured review exchanges. Before joining any site, study its policies carefully—especially regarding retailer guidelines—to ensure compliance with platforms like Amazon.

There are clear advantages to using reputable review sites.

First, they reduce the time required to find interested readers. Instead of cold pitching individuals, you list your book within a system already populated with readers actively seeking titles to review.

Second, they can accelerate early review accumulation, which is particularly useful at launch when social proof is minimal.

Third, they provide structure—deadlines, tracking dashboards, and automated reminders—which can increase follow-through rates.

However, there are limitations and risks to consider. Reviews obtained through paid platforms may not carry the same audience exposure as influencer posts. A review left quietly on a retail site does not necessarily generate traffic beyond its immediate placement.

Additionally, costs can add up, especially if results are inconsistent. Some readers may download an ARC and never post a review, depending on the platform's enforcement mechanisms.

There is also a perception factor. While using paid ARC distribution services is common and legitimate when handled ethically, you must avoid any arrangement that incentivizes only positive reviews.

Authenticity is critical. Retailers penalize manipulation, and readers quickly detect inflated praise patterns.

In evaluating whether to use these platforms, apply the same ROI framework discussed earlier. Are you gaining review volume? Are those reviews detailed and thoughtful? Is your average rating improving? Are you building an email list or reader community alongside review growth?

Paid platforms are tools. They are not replacements for long-term relationship building with bloggers and influencers.

Used strategically, they can supplement your outreach efforts and provide foundational social proof—especially for newer authors without established networks.

Measuring ROI When Payment Isn't Money

In traditional advertising, ROI is measured in dollars spent versus dollars earned.

In reviewer outreach, the transaction is less direct. You are often offering free copies and time in exchange for exposure and credibility. That doesn't mean ROI is immeasurable—it simply requires broader thinking.

The first layer is social proof. Reviews increase buyer confidence. Even a modest number of thoughtful reviews can improve conversion rates on retail platforms.

Monitor how review count and average rating evolve over time. Capture compelling review excerpts for use in newsletters, on your website, and in promotional graphics.

The second layer is visibility. When a blogger features your book or an influencer post about it, you may see temporary increases in website traffic, social media followers, or newsletter subscriptions. Use trackable links when possible so you can connect exposure to measurable behavior.

The third layer is relationship capital. A positive experience with one blogger may lead to coverage for future releases, interviews, giveaways, or collaborations. Influencer relationships compound. A single strong partnership can outlast dozens of cold pitches.

The fourth later is insight. Reviews reveal how readers interpret your story. Which elements resonate? Which themes stand out? Sometimes reviewers articulate your book's strengths more clearly than your own marketing copy does. That is valuable intelligence.

ROI in this space is often delayed. A review posted today may influence a purchase months from now. Do not measure success solely by immediate sales spikes. Look for patterns over time. If you treat reviews purely as transactional sales tools, you will miss their strategic value. They are reputation builders.

Action Plan: Building Your Reviewer System

1. **Identify Genre-Aligned Reviewers:** Create a focused list of blogs, Instagram or TikTok accounts, newsletters, and other platforms relevant to your book. Prioritize accounts with consistent recent activity and engaged audiences. Document everything in a tracking system so each contact is measurable.

2. **Refine Your Outreach Template:** Draft a concise, adaptable template that can be personalized efficiently for each reviewer. Tailor the opening and fit statement for each contact, keeping the core message consistent.

3. **Limit Weekly Outreach for Manageability:** Send outreach in manageable batches each week to ensure prompt responses and maintain staggered visibility. Avoid mass outreach that overwhelms your ability to follow up.

4. **Test Paid Review Platforms Selectively:** If your budget allows, try one reputable paid review platform with a single campaign first. Track the number, quality, and timing of reviews received. Compare results to direct outreach to determine ROI.

5. **Track Responses Objectively:** Record acceptances, declines, and non-responses without emotional reaction. After several weeks as: Which types of accounts respond most often? Which platforms generate the strongest engagement?

6. **Monitor Broader Impact:** Track new reviews, collect standout quotes, and observe changes in traffic, follower growth, or subscriber increases. Even small upward trends indicate momentum.

7. **Commit to Consistency:** Treat outreach as on ongoing marketing activity, not a one-time launch task. Regular engagement with influencers,

blogs, and review platforms builds long-term credibility and amplifies your reach over time.

Focus on strategy, tracking, and consistency. Credibility builds gradually—but when all pieces align, growth looks sudden and organic.

PART V – Post-Launch
Keeping Your Book Alive

Chapter Fifteen

What to Do After Launch Week Ends

Launch week is intense by design. It demands focus, coordination, and energy. You show up everywhere. You email your list. You post daily. You ask for reviews. You monitor numbers. For a brief window, your book feels like the center of your professional universe.

Then the week ends.

The inbox quiets. The adrenaline drops. And many authors, exhausted from the push, unintentionally step away from promotion altogether. Not because they lack commitment—but because they believe the main event is over.

This is where most books begin to fade.

Why Most Books Die Quietly After Launch

Books rarely disappear because they are poorly written. They disappear because attention disappears. The promotional engine that was running at full speed suddenly shuts off. Visibility declines. Conversations shift. The book, still valuable and relevant, simply stops being mentioned.

What authors often misunderstand is that launch week primarily reaches the people who were already paying attention. You email subscribers, your close followers, your immediate network—they are the first wave. But there are many more potential readers who were not watching during that week. Some had not yet discovered you. Some saw the announcement and meant to return but did not. Others need repeated exposure before they act.

When you stop talking about your book, you unintentionally signal that it's no longer important. Audiences take their cues from you. If the author moves on quickly, readers assume the moment has passed.

Publishing is not a one-week event. It is an ongoing campaign. Launch week introduces your book to the market. The months that follow determine whether it becomes a short-term spike or a long-term asset.

Creating a Post-Launch Promotion Plan

The shift after launch should not be from "promotion" to "silence." It should be from intensity to sustainability.

Without a plan, authors promote randomly. They mention the book when inspiration strikes or when sales dip. This inconsistency leads to unpredictable results and unnecessary stress. Instead, what you need is a structured but manageable system that keeps your book visible without recreating the pressure of launch week.

Begin by integrating your book into your regular content. Your book should not sit on a shelf, separate from your daily messaging. It should become the foundation of your teaching. Each chapter likely contains multiple ideas that can stand alone as lessons. Those lessons can be shared as articles, short posts, emails, videos, or workshop segments. When you teach from your book, you reinforce your authority while gently reminding your audience that a deeper resource exists.

You are not repeating yourself when you reference your book. You are reinforcing a message. Repetition, in marketing, is clarity. Most people need to hear an idea multiple times before it becomes memorable.

In addition to ongoing content integration, schedule periodic promotional waves. These are no relaunches. They are focused periods of attention. You might choose to spotlight your book for one week each quarter, align it with a seasonal theme, or connect it to an industry event. By planning these waves in advance, you prevent the book from drifting out of sight.

Post-launch is also the ideal time to expand your reach beyond your existing audience. When the urgency of launch week has passed, you can pursue podcast interviews, guest articles, and speaking engagements with more strategy and less pressure. You are no longer asking others to support a narrow deadline. You are offering expertise supported by a published work. That positioning carries weight.

How Often Should You Promote After Launch?

Many authors fear overpromotion. They worry about appearing repetitive or overly focused on sales. As a result, they under-promote.

The reality is that your audience changes constantly. New subscribers join. New followers discover you. People who missed earlier posts encounter you for the first time. What feels repetitive to you is often brand new to them.

After launch, promotion should become rhythmic rather than intense. Your book should be mentioned regularly—woven into conversations, teaching, and examples. Direct promotional reminders can appear periodically, while subtle references can appear more frequently. The goal is not to dominate every message with a sales pitch. The goal is to normalize the presence of your book within your brand.

Consistency build familiarity. Familiarity builds trust. Trust leads to sales.

If months pass without you mentioning your book, you are relying on chance instead of strategy.

Refreshing Your Book's Visibility Without Relaunching

One common mistake authors make is believing that renewed attention requires another large-scale launch. It does not. What it requires is a fresh angle.

Your book contains multiple promises. During launch week, you likely emphasized one primary benefit. Afterward, you can highlight others. Perhaps the book serves as a practical guide, but it also offers mindset shifts, time-saving frameworks, or confidence-building strategies.

By adjusting the emphasis, you create renewed interest without changing the product.

Reader experiences are another powerful way to refresh visibility. Testimonials, case studies, and success stories shift the focus away from you and toward transformation.

When prospective readers see evidence that others have benefited, the book regains urgency. Social proof breathes life into a message that might otherwise feel familiar.

You can also expand your book's ecosystem. Companion resources such as checklists, workbooks, bonus trainings, or live discussions provide new entry points for readers.

These additions do not require rewriting the book. They require re-engaging with its material in creative ways. Each new piece of content becomes another pathway leading back to the original work.

Finally, context matters. A book that seemed general at launch may become highly relevant when connected to current trends, industry shifts, or seasonal challenges. By framing your message within what is happening now, you keep it timely. Timeliness creates renewed curiosity.

Embracing the Long-Term View

Launch week creates noise. Post-launch creates stability.

The authors who build lasting careers understand that a book is intellectual property, not temporary content. It can generate leads, open speaking opportunities, support courses, strengthen credibility, and produce ongoing revenue. But only if it remains visible.

Promotion after launch is not about chasing numbers. It's about stewardship. You invested time, research, and creativity into your book. Continuing to promote it ensures that effort continues to serve people.

Momentum is rarely dramatic after launch week. It is built quietly through consistent effort. A mention in a newsletter. A quote in a post. A lesson drawn from a chapter. An interview that reaches a new audience. These actions compound over time.

Your book does not need another grand opening. It needs sustained attention.

Action Step: Build a 90-Day Post-Launch Visibility Plan (Step-by-Step)

1. Audit Your Book for Promotional Assets: Review your book's table of contents and identify the teachable moments inside. Write down your book's core promise, 10-20 key ideas, frameworks, or step-by-step processes, stories, examples, or case studies that resonate with readers. This becomes your **content bank.** Most authors underestimate how much material is ready to use.

2. Turn Ideas into Weekly Touchpoints: Open your calendar and plan 12 weeks of content, one idea per week. Each piece can be a newsletter topic, short social media posts or series, live teaching sessions, blog articles or short-form videos, workshop segments. Be specific. For example: "Teach Framework from Chapter 3" or "Share client story from Chapter 5." At the end of each piece, naturally reference your book as the deeper resource.

3. Schedule Three Focused Spotlight Weeks: Choose three weeks in the 90-day period for slightly elevated book promotion—one per month. During each week, you might send one dedicated email about the book, share 2-3 posts highlighting benefits or testimonials, offer a limited-time bonus (checklist, download, resource), host a short Q&A or live session. Put these weeks on your calendar—treat them as non-negotiable appointments.

4. Identify Two External Visibility Opportunities: Plan outreach beyond your current audience. Examples: pitch three podcasts, submit a guest article, contact an organization about speaking, or propose a workshop based on your book's framework. Write down exact names and assign deadlines to ensure follow-through.

5. Choose a Fresh Angle for Promotion: Decide how you will reposition your book during these 90 days. **Ask:** What problem does this book solve that wasn't emphasized at launch? What new type of reader could benefit? What result deserves more attention? Write one clear sentence to frame this new emphasis. **Examples:** *"This book is a decision-making system, not just a guide."* Or *"This book helps professionals reduce overwhelm in under 30 days."* This fresh angle will guide your messaging during spotlight weeks.

What This Plan Accomplishes:

- 12 weeks of pre-planned content

- 3 intentional visibility pushes

- 2 external outreach goals

- A refreshed promotional angle

Consistency keeps your book visible long after launch. Once this 90-day plan ends, repeat the process—books remain relevant when authors remain consistent.

Chapter Sixteen

Long-Term Visibility Strategies

Launch week creates noise. Long-term visibility creates income. Most authors pour enormous energy into their launch and then quietly hope momentum will continue on its own.

Sometimes it does—for a short while. But sustainable visibility does not happen by accident. It happens because the author treats the book as an ongoing asset rather than a finished event.

A published book is not static. The market changes. Categories grow more competitive. Cover trends evolve. Reader expectations shift. Even Amazon's internal systems adjust over time.

If you want your book to remain visible and competitive, you must revisit it periodically with the mindset of a strategist, not just a creator.

Long-term visibility is not about constantly shouting. It is about making smart, well-timed adjustments that keep your book relevant without exhausting your audience—or yourself.

Using KDP Dashboard Promotions Strategically

One of the most powerful long-term visibility tools is built directly into your KDP dashboard. Many authors either ignore these tools or use them impulsively. Both approaches leave opportunity on the table.

If your eBook is enrolled in KDP Select, Amazon provides several promotional options designed to increase discoverability for limited windows of time. These include Kindle Countdown Deals, Free Book Promotions, Kindle Deal nominations, and exposure through Prime Reading or Kindle Unlimited Programs.

The key word here is limited. These tools are not meant to permanently alter your pricing. They are designed to create temporary surges in visibility.

When used intentionally, they allow you to reintroduce your book to the marketplace months—or even years—after launch.

Kindle Countdown Deals: Creating Urgency Without Losing Value

A Kindle Countdown Deal allows you to temporarily discount your eBook while displaying a visible countdown timer on your Amazon product page. Readers can see the current promotional price, the original price, and exactly how much time remains before the price increases again.

This structure matters more than many authors realize.

The presence of the timer shifts the psychology of the purchase. Instead of appearing like a quiet price drop, the promotion feels like a timed opportunity. Urgency increases without damaging perceived value because readers know the discount is temporary.

Another advantage is that you continue earning royalties based on the discounted price in eligible marketplaces. That means you are not sacrificing all revenue in exchange for exposure.

Countdown Deals work especially well when you are trying to boost rankings quickly, support advertising campaigns, promote a sequel, or reignite momentum after a slow period. They can also be effective when tied to a seasonal theme that naturally aligns with your book's topic.

However, frequency matters. If readers begin to expect a countdown every month, the urgency disappears. The tool loses its power. Used sparingly and with clear intention, it can create meaningful spikes in visibility.

Free Book Promotions: Reach Over Revenue

KDP Select allows authors to offer their eBook for free for up to five days during each 90-day enrollment period. On the surface, this seems simple: set the price to zero and watch downloads increase.

And downloads usually do increase—sometimes dramatically.

Free removes friction. It encourages impulse decisions. It expands reach quickly. Your book can climb category charts in the free rankings and gain exposure to readers who might never have taken a chance on an unfamiliar author.

But free downloads are not the same as engaged readers.

When someone pays even a small amount for a book, they have made a commitment. When a book is free, that commitment disappears. Many free downloads sit unread on digital shelves.

For this reason, free promotions are most powerful when your book connects to something larger. If it is the first in a series, free days can drive read-through to later books. If your book includes a strong call-to-action to join your email list, free promotions can expand your audience. If you offer services, courses, or speaking engagements, free access can function as a lead generator.

Free should not be used casually. It should be used strategically, with a clear plan for what happens after the promotion ends.

When treated as part of a funnel rather than a revenue event, free can be remarkably effective.

Kindle Deals: Platform-Driven Visibility

In addition to self-scheduled promotions, Amazon occasionally allows authors to nominate up to two books at a time for curated Kindle Deal promotions.

These are not guaranteed placements. Amazon reviews nominated titles and selects books it believes will perform well in a broader promotional campaign. If accepted, your book may receive enhanced visibility beyond your own marketing efforts.

This is significant because platform-driven exposure carries weight. Amazon's internal promotions can introduce your book to readers outside your immediate audience.

However, selection tends to favor books with strong reviews, consistent sales history, professional covers, and competitive metadata. In other words, your foundation must already be solid.

You cannot rely on Kindle Deals as a strategy. But when the opportunity appears, you should be prepared to take advantage of it.

Think of this as allowing the platform to amplify your existing momentum.

Prime Reading and Subscription Visibility

Prime Reading and Kindle Unlimited programs introduce your book to readers who may not purchase it outright but are active within Amazon's subscription ecosystem.

For some authors, particularly those writing in genre fiction or multi-book series, page reads through subscription programs can generate steady income and increase exposure simultaneously.

The primary benefit here is discoverability. Readers browsing within Prime or Kindle Unlimited often experiment with new authors because the perceived risk is lower. That exposure can lead to read-through across a series or future purchases.

However, this approach requires comfort with trading margin for reach. Subscription-based visibility is most powerful when you have multiple books availability. One standalone title may benefit from exposure, but a connected catalog multiples the impact.

A Sample Post-Launch Promotion Timeline

Imagine the first year after your book launches.

In the first two months, you focus on stability. You allow reviews to accumulate. You optimize your metadata. You monitor how readers respond. You resist the temptation to discount immediately. Your regular price establishes confidence and value.

Around month three, once your foundation is stable, you run your first Kindle Countdown Deal. You promote it to your email list and possibly support it with light advertising.

The goal is to increase rankings and attract new readers while preserving perceived value.

Several months later, perhaps around month five or six, you schedule a short Free Book Promotion. This time, you are prepared. Your back matter includes a compelling invitation to join your newsletter. If your book is part of a series, the next installment is already available. You are not simply giving the book away—you are guiding readers somewhere.

Later in the year, if your reviews and sales performance are strong, you nominate your book for a Kindle Deal when the opportunity becomes available. You maintain your normal marketing activities, but you allow for the possibility of platform amplification.

As the year progresses, you may align a short Countdown Deal with a seasonal moment that naturally connects to your book's theme.

A productivity book fits well with New Year goal-setting. A financial guide aligns with tax season. A leadership book may resonate during corporate performance review cycles.

Each promotion has a purpose. Each one connects to a broader strategy. None of them are random.

That is the difference between noise and momentum.

Protecting Value While Increasing Visibility

Price is a signal. Your regular price communicates how you value your own work.

When you discount with intention, the promotion feels like a limited opportunity. When you discount frequently and without structure, the lower price becomes your identity.

Readers are perceptive. If they believe your book is constantly "on sale," the simply wait.

The goal is not constant promotion. It is strategic bursts of attention that return to a stable baseline.

Your book is intellectual property It deserves to be treated like a long-term asset, not a clearance item.

Updating Covers, Blurbs, and Metadata

Promotions bring traffic. Packaging converts it.

If readers land on your product page during a promotion and your cover appears outdated compared to others in your category, conversion suffers.

The same is true if your blurb buries the strongest benefit or fails to clearly articulate the transformation your reader will experience.

Markets evolve. Design trends shift. New subcategories emerge. Terminology changes. Revisiting your cover, description, keywords, and categories periodically ensures your book remains competitive.

This does not mean reinventing your brand every year. It means refining it.

Small improvements in conversion rates compound over time. Even a modest increase in page-to-purchase conversion can dramatically affect long-term revenue.

The Compounding Effect of Strategic Stewardship

One promotion increases rankings temporarily.

One metadata update improves discoverability.

One cover refresh strengthens first impressions.

One seasonal campaign renews relevance.

Individually, these actions may appear minor. Collectively, they create sustained visibility.

The authors who maintain long-term sales are rarely the loudest voices in the room. They are the most attentive. They monitor performance. They refine positioning. They adjust based on data rather than emotion.

Long-term visibility is not luck. It is stewardship.

Your launch introduced your book to the world. Your ongoing strategy determines whether the world continues to see it.

Treat your book like something meant to last—and it just might.

Action Steps: Strengthen Your Long-Term Visibility Plan

1. **Adopt a Publisher's Perspective:** Set aside a focused session and view your book as a product you are responsible for growing. Emotional attachment is natural; strategic distance is powerful.

2. **Review Pricing History and Promotions:** Look back over the last six months. Ask: Did each promotion have a clear objective? (Boost reviews, rankings, email subscribers, or traffic?); Were any actions reactive rather than intentional? Note what worked, what didn't, and why. If you haven't run promotions yet, plan one intentional window within the next 90 days and define its purpose first.

3. **Examine Available Promotional Tools:** Check your KDP dashboard or other retailer tools. Review remaining Countdown or Free days (if enrolled in KDP Select). Consider how each tool would fit into a larger visibility plan. Draft a follow-up strategy for new readers before scheduling any promotions.

4. **Audit Your Product Page:** Look at your cover compared with top-selling books in your category. Does it visually single genre and topic? Check your blurb—focus on the first three lines. Are they compelling and clear? Even small improvements can boost conversions.

5. **Update Metadata Thoughtfully:** Research your categories and keywords as they exist today. Are there better subcategories now? Has niche terminology evolved? Make careful, deliberate improvements rather than multiple rushed changes.

6. **Map Out the Next Six Months:** Create a simple calendar and identify at least two seasonal or industry moments that connect naturally to your book. Plan light promotional pushes, content, or messaging around these moments in advance.

7. **Focus on Stewardship, Not Constant Activity:** Your goal is ongoing care. Monitor performance without panic. Make measured adjustments instead of impulsive ones. Update covers, metadata, and descriptions when needed. Use promotions intentionally, not desperately.

8. Think in Terms of Longevity: Ask "How can this book remain competitive and relevant for years?" Shift from urgency to ownership. A launch is a moment; stewardship is a practice.

Consistent, strategic attention keeps your book alive and relevant long after launch week. Stewardship turns your book from a single event into a lasting asset.

Chapter Seventeen

Writing in a Series—The Best Marketing Strategy

There is a truth in publishing that feels almost *unfair* when you first hear it: the best way to sell your first book is to write your second.

And then your third.

And then your fourth.

While marketing tactics matter, while ads can help, while covers and blurbs absolutely influence buying decisions, nothing outperforms a well-structured series when it comes to long-term revenue and visibility.

A single book can generate income. A series can generate momentum.

When a reader finishes a satisfying book, they experience what psychologists call "narrative transportation." They have invested emotionally. They have bonded with characters or trusted your expertise. They want continuity. They want more.

If you do not provide it, they move on to another author who does.

Series writing is not simply a creative choice. It is one of the most powerful marketing strategies available to an author.

Why Series Sell Better Than Standalones

A standalone book asks a reader to take one risk. A series rewards that risk with ongoing familiarity.

From a buyer's perspective, discovering a new author involves uncertainty. Will the writing style resonate? Will the story deliver? Will the advice be useful? Purchasing book one requires trust.

If the reader enjoys that first experience, the trust barrier disappears for the next purchase. The emotional investment is already made. The world is already familiar. The author has already proven competence.

This is why series dramatically increase lifetime customer value. Instead of earning revenue from a single transaction, you create a pathway for multiple purchases from the same reader.

Acquiring a new reader is often the most difficult and expensive part of marketing. A series allows you to maximize the return on that initial acquisition.

Retail algorithms also favor series. When a reader purchases book one and quickly moves to book two, it signals engagement. Engagement signals relevance. Relevance strengthens visibility. The system recognizes patterns of read-through and rewards books that keep readers on the platform.

Beyond the algorithm, there is the psychological component. Humans crave continuity.

In fiction, readers want to revisit characters they care about. In nonfiction, readers want progressive mastery. A business book that solves one problem naturally opens the door to deeper strategies. A wellness guide that addresses mindset can lead into habits, nutrition, or productivity.

A series creates a journey rather than a single event.

And journeys keep people moving forward.

Structuring a Series for Maximum Read-Through

Writing multiple books is not enough. Structure determines whether readers continue or quietly exit after one book.

In fiction, each installment must provide a satisfying arc while leaving enough unresolved threads to create anticipation. Readers should feel rewarded, not manipulated.

A cliffhanger can be powerful, but only if the primary emotional contract of the book has been honored. If readers feel tricked into buying the next book simply to receive closure, trust erodes.

A stronger strategy is layered resolution. The central conflict of the current book resolves in a meaningful way, but a larger narrative thread continues to unfold. This creates forward momentum without frustration.

In nonfiction, structuring for read-through requires intentional sequencing. Each book should solve a distinct but related problem. Book one may address foundations. Book two may build on implementation. Book three may explore advanced strategy or case studies.

When each title feels both complete and connected, readers naturally progress.

Clarity is essential. The series order should be obvious on the cover, in the subtitle, and in the product description. Confusion kills read-through. If readers cannot easily determine which book comes next, many will not take the time to figure it out.

The final pages of each book play a critical role. A compelling invitation to continue the journey—clearly introducing the next title and explaining what it offers—dramatically increases conversion. Do not assume readers will search for it. Guide them directly.

A well-structured series feels intentional from beginning to end. It does not feel accidental. It does not feel loosely connected. It feels like a roadmap.

Promoting Book One as the Gateway

In a series strategy, book one carries disproportionate importance. It is the entry point. The gateway. The introduction to your voice and value.

For this reason, book one often becomes the primary promotional focus, even after multiple books are published.

Many successful authors price book one lower than the rest of the series, occasionally discount it, or use promotional tools to increase visibility.

The goal is not to maximize revenue from book one. The goal is to maximize entry into the ecosystem.

If a reader moves from book one to book two and beyond, the initial discount becomes an investment rather than a loss.

This is where long-term thinking separates strategic authors from reactive ones.

Instead of asking, "How much can I earn from this one book?" the question becomes, "How many readers can I bring into the series?"

Advertising efforts often perform better when directed toward book one because the potential return is multiplied across future sales. A reader who enjoys your writing does not require convincing twice.

The presentation of book one must be especially strong. The cover should align clearly with the genre or category. The blurb must communicate both immediate value and the promise of continuation. Reviews on book one carry extra weight because they influence the entire series pipeline.

In many ways, book one functions less like a single product and more like a storefront.

Its job is to invite readers inside.

Rapid Release vs. Sustainable Writing Schedules

Once authors understand the power of series, the next question often becomes how quickly to publish the installments.

Rapid release strategies involve publishing multiple books in a short time frame, sometimes spacing them only weeks apart.

This approach can generate significant momentum because readers do not have to wait long between installments. Marketing efforts compound. Visibility remains concentrated. The algorithm registers sustained activity.

However, rapid release requires preparation. Writing several books before launching the first is often necessary to maintain quality and meet deadlines. Without preparation, the pressure can compromise craft, increase stress, and lead to burnout.

On the other hand, a sustainable schedule prioritizes consistency over speed. Books may release every six months or annually. While momentum builds more gradually, this pace allows for thoughtful development, stronger editing, and long-term career sustainability.

Neither approach is universally superior. The appropriate strategy depends on your genre, your capacity, your resources, and your long-term goals.

The danger lies in choosing a schedule based on comparison rather than alignment.

Publishing is a marathon, not a sprint. If rapid release compromises quality or well-being, the short-term visibility boost may not justify the long-term cost.

Readers ultimately care about one thing above all else: delivering a satisfying experience. Whether you publish quickly or steadily, protecting that experience must remain the priority.

The Compounding Power of Continuation

A series transforms marketing from constant acquisition into progressive retention.

Instead of repeatedly convincing strangers to trust you, you nurture readers who already have.

Each new release strengthens the entire catalog.

Each installment increases the earning potential of the previous ones.

Book three sells book one just as much as book one sells book three.

This is the compounding effect that makes series so powerful. The catalog becomes interconnected. Visibility circulates internally. Your marketing efforts no longer point to a single destination but to an expanding ecosystem.

For many authors, the breakthrough moment does not come with their first book. It arrives when their third, fourth, or fifth book creates enough gravitational pull to lift the earlier titles.

That is when the strategy becomes visible.

Writing in a series is not merely a creative decision. It is a structural advantage. It is a way of building assets that support one another. It is the difference between opening a single shop and building a network of connected locations.

And if your goal is long-term visibility, stable income, and a growing readership, there are a few strategies more effective than giving your readers somewhere to go next.

Because when a reader closes one book and immediately opens another with your name on it, marketing has already done its job.

Action Steps: Build Your Series Strategy

1. **Evaluate Series Potential:** Before writing another book, determine if your current book—or your idea—can expand naturally into a series without feeling stretched. **Fiction:** Does your world have depth beyond one story? Are there secondary characters or larger conflicts worth exploring? **Nonfiction:** Can your topic be broken into stages of mastery—foundations, application, advanced strategies, case studies, or specialization?

2. **Sketch a Three-Book Arc:** Define the role each book will play in the reader's journey. Clarity now prevents series sprawl later. **Book One:** Introduce transformation. **Book Two:** Deepen or complicate that transformation. **Book Three:** Show progression without repetition.

3. **Design Your Read-Through Intentionally:** Review your current book's back matter. Is there a clear invitation to continue? Does it introduce the next book specifically and explain reader benefits? Rewrite if needed to guide readers naturally to the next installment.

4. **Decide on a Publishing Pace:** Assess your schedule, energy, and commitments. Can you write multiple books before releasing the first? Or is a steady, sustainable cadence better for quality and sanity? Choose a timeline that aligns with your real life—not someone else's highlight reel.

5. **Strengthen Your Marketing Focus:** If you already have multiple books, ensure book one is the clear entry point, check for cohesive covers across the series, confirm the order is unmistakable, align pricing to encourage readers to begin. Book one should act as a gateway, not just another title.

6. **Shift to Catalog Thinking:** Write down how many books you want in this series over the next 3-5 years. Seeing your work as an interconnected body of work—not isolated projects—sharpens strategy and decision-making.

<u>The Goal:</u> Your next book is not just another product—it's leverage. Series thinking turns each release into compounding momentum and long-term visibility.

PART VI – Scaling, Repeating, and Not Burning Out

Chapter Eighteen

Creating a Repeatable Promotion System

I f there is one lesson I have learned the hard way in my author journey, it is this: ambition is not the problem. The absence of margin is.

For years, I approached promotion the way many self-published authors do. I would get inspired, build an elaborate plan, execute it intensely for a season, and then watch it unravel the moment life shifted. I told myself I just needed to be more disciplined. More focused. More committed.

What I actually needed was a repeatable system—one that could survive real life.

Over the last year, I decided to treat my author career like a business with structure instead of a creative project fueled by motivation. I built a full publishing calendar with one book scheduled every other month, complete with launch timelines. I launched a private Facebook group for self-published authors. I started a podcast called *From Writer to Author: The Podcast.* I began writing weekly blog posts that aligned with each episode. I created a social media schedule that required me to post in both my private Facebook group and my official author page. I began developing an online course for self-published authors. And all the while, I continued serving my editing, formatting, and coaching clients.

On paper, it was impressive. In practice, it was intense.

For nearly a year, I kept up with it. I was proud of the consistency. I proved to myself that I could build momentum across multiple platforms. I created structure where chaos used to live.

And then life stepped in—in a good way.

My husband is retiring, and we are in the process of moving from one state to another. What that means in reality is home repairs, preparing the house to sell, packing, searching for a new home, paperwork, decisions, travel, and the emotional energy that comes with transition. None of it is negative. It is simply full.

And fullness requires adjustment.

Recently, everything came to a head. I was trying to keep up with weekly podcast episodes, weekly blog posts, daily social media posts, course creation, client work, book writing, book launches, and house projects. I was technically capable of doing it all. But capability and sustainability are not the same thing.

I realized something critical: I had built a schedule that left no room for "life stuff" or physical energy limits. My ambition was strong. My margin was nonexistent.

So, I made a decision.

Just this week, I began temporarily paring things down. My podcast will no longer release weekly—for now. Because the blog aligns with the podcast, it will also pause its weekly rhythm. My online course creation is moving to the back burner until after the move. Instead, I am concentrating on what truly moves the needle in this season: writing my books and keeping my publishing schedule, launching those books well, serving my clients with excellence, and posting once or twice a week instead of daily.

There was nothing wrong with my original vision. But the system needed retooling.

That is what this chapter is about.

Building a Promotion Calendar You'll Actually Follow

When authors create promotion calendars, they often build them for their best-case selves. The version of themselves with unlimited energy, uninterrupted focus, and perfectly predictable weeks.

That version does not exist.

A calendar you will actually follow must be built around your real life, not your ideal one. It must include margin. It must allow for illness, travel, family needs, unexpected opportunities, and simple human fatigue.

When I created my year-long plan, I accounted for output but not for interruption. I scheduled books, launches, podcasts, blogs, social posts, and course creation—but I did not schedule recovery time. I did not build in slower seasons. I did not ask, "What happens if something changes?"

A sustainable promotion calendar answers three questions clearly:

1. What are my core priorities?

2. What directly supports book sales and long-term growth?

3. What can flex when needed?

For me, the non-negotiables right now are writing and launching my books, and serving my clients. Those are revenue-driving and mission-critical. The podcast, blog, and course creation are valuable, but they are expandable and contractible. They can stretch or shrink depending on season.

Your calendar must reflect your hierarchy of importance.

Instead of stacking everything at maximum capacity, build layers:

- **Core layer:** Writing, publishing schedule, direct audience communication.

- **Growth layer:** Authority-building content like podcasts, blogs, collaborations.

- **Expansion layer:** New courses, experimental platforms, additional projects.

When life intensifies, you trim from the outer layers inward—not from the core.

That is how you build something you can actually maintain.

Tracking What Works and Ditching What Doesn't

One of the reasons it felt safe for me to scale back is because I had been paying attention to what truly mattered.

Tracking is not about obsessing over numbers. It is about understanding cause and effect. When you know what produces results, you can confidently release what does not.

Over the last year, I noticed that my book launches—when done with focused attention—produced measurable growth. Consistent communication with my email list mattered. Serving my clients well strengthened referrals and long-term stability.

Daily posting on social media? It built visibility, yes. But it did not produce results proportional to the time and energy required during this heavy season.

When you track what works, scaling back becomes strategic instead of emotional.

Each month, evaluate:

- What directly increased sales or subscribers?

- What deepened relationship with readers?

- What consumed energy without measurable return?

Ditching what does not serve your long-term growth is not failure. It is maturity. A system improves through subtraction as much as through addition.

Small Actions That Compound Over Time

Here is the truth that keeps m steady: small, consistent actions compound far more effectively than bursts of intensity.

Publishing one book every other month may not feel dramatic in isolation. But across a year, that is six new titles. Across several years, that becomes a substantial catalog. A catalog builds credibility. Credibility builds trust. Trust builds sales.

Posting once or twice a week consistently for years is more powerful than posting daily for a season and disappearing the next.

The key is sustainability.

Compounding works only when actions are repeatable. That is why I am not abandoning my promotional efforts; I am resizing them. I am protecting the actions that I can sustain long-term.

You must think beyond this month. Beyond this launch. Beyond this season.

Ask yourself: Can I maintain this rhythm for a year? If not, adjust it until the answer is yes.

Turning Promotion Into Habit Instead of Panic

Earlier in my career, promotion was reactive. If sales dipped, I scrambled. If a launch approached, I overextended. It felt urgent and emotional.

What changes over the last year was structure. Having a publishing calendar, launch timelines, scheduled posts, and recurring tasks reduced decision fatigue. I no longer asked, "What should I do today?" I simply followed the system.

Now, even while scaling back, I am not operating from panic. I am operating from adjustment.

Habits are not about rigidity. They are about predictability. When promotion becomes habitual, you can shrink or expand it without losing stability.

Right now, my habit is simple:

- Write the books.

- Launch them intentionally.

- Serve my clients.

- Show up online once or twice a week.

- Communicate consistently with my audience.

It is quieter than before. But it is stable.

And stability builds careers.

Ambition Needs Margin to Thrive

Your ambition is not the enemy. It never was. The drive to write more books, reach more readers, build more platforms, and create more opportunities is not something you need to suppress. It is evidence that you care deeply about your calling. It is the spark that pushed you to publish in the first place.

But ambition without margin becomes pressure. And pressure, sustained long enough, becomes burnout.

Margin is not laziness. It is wisdom. It is the space between what you *could* do and what you *choose* to do. It is the breathing room that allows you to adjust when life shifts, when energy dips, when unexpected opportunities arise, or when responsibilities increase.

In my own journey, I learned this lesson by building something that technically worked—but only under perfect conditions. For nearly a year, I proved I could maintain an aggressive publishing schedule, a weekly podcast, a weekly blog, daily social media engagement, client work, and course development. The system held... until life required more of me physically and emotionally.

Nothing went wrong. In fact, good things happened. A retirement. A move. A transition into a new season. But those good things required energy. Time. Focus. And because I had filled every available space in my schedule, something had to give.

That is when I realized an important truth: a system that only works when life is quiet is not a strong system.

Margin is what allows ambition to survive transition.

When you build space into your calendar—buffer weeks between launches, realistic posting schedule, flexible creative timelines—you are not lowering your standards. You are protecting your longevity. You are choosing to build a career that lasts years, not one that burns brightly for a season and then exhausts you.

Consider the difference between sprinting and distance running. Sprinting requires explosive effort and delivers short bursts of speed. Distance running requires pacing, rhythm, and endurance. A writing career is not a sprint. It is an endurance race. And endurance demands margin.

Margin also protects your creativity. When every hour is assigned and every task feels urgent, creativity becomes mechanical. Writing turns into output instead of inspiration. Promotion turns into obligation instead of connection. But when you leave space—white space on the calendar, white space in your mind—you give ideas room to breathe.

You cannot think strategically when you are constantly reacting.

The authors who sustain long-term success are not the ones who do the most at once. They are the ones who build systems flexible enough to absorb change. They expect interruptions. They plan for slower seasons. They design promotion schedules that can contract when necessary and expand when possible.

Margin is not the opposite of ambition. It is the structure that makes ambition sustainable.

So, as you build your repeatable promotion system, ask yourself a different question. Instead of asking, "How much can I fit in?" ask, "What pace can I maintain with excellence for the next three years?"

That question changes everything.

Because when you build with margin, you do not have to start over every time life shifts. You adjust. You refine. You continue.

Ambition built on margin does not collapse under pressure. It adapts. It steadies. It endures.

And that is the kind of ambition that builds a career worth keeping.

Action Steps: Retool Your Promotion System

Before you move on to the next chapter, take time to implement these steps thoughtfully.

1. **Audit Your Current Commitments:** Write down everything you are currently doing for promotion and growth. Be honest. Seeing it on paper often reveals why you feel stretched.

2. **Identify Your Core Priorities:** Circle the activities that directly generate income or significantly grow your readership. These stay.

3. **Temporarily Release One Outer-Layer Activity:** Choose one growth or expansive activity that can pause without harming your long-term goals. Remove it from your schedule for the next 60-90 days.

4. **Build Margin Into Your Calendar:** Add buffer weeks between launches. Reduce posting frequency if necessary. Schedule recovery time after major pushes.

5. **Create a Sustainable Weekly Rhythm:** Design a promotional schedule you can maintain even during stressful seasons. Test it for one month and adjust as needed.

6. **Commit to Quarterly Retooling:** Your life will change. Your energy will shift. Your business will evolve. Schedule time every quarter to reassess and refine your system.

Chapter Nineteen

What Successful Indie Authors Do Differently

When people look at successful indie authors from the outside, they often assume there is a secret strategy, a hidden platform, or a lucky break that explains their results.

There usually isn't.

What separates sustainable indie success from stalled effort is rarely talent alone. It is rarely one viral post. It is rarely one big launch. More often than not, the difference lies in quiet disciplines practiced consistently over time.

Successful indie authors think differently about visibility, growth, and momentum. They are less distracted by short-term noise and more committed to long-term stability. They understand that publishing is not a single event—it is an ecosystem.

Let's look closely at what they do differently.

Consistency Over Virality

Virality is seductive. It promises rapid growth, instant recognition, and a sudden influx of readers. In a digital world that rewards spikes of attention, it is easy to believe that one viral moment will change everything.

But sustainable careers are not built on spikes. They are built on patterns.

Successful indie authors prioritize consistency over virality because they understand a simple truth: visibility that can be repeated is more valuable than visibility that cannot.

A viral post might gain thousands of views. But if it does not connect to a consistent system—an email list, a book catalog, a reader funnel—those views fade as quickly as they arrive.

In contrast, posting regularly, communicating steadily with readers, and releasing books on a predictable schedule creates reliability. Readers begin to expect you. Algorithms begin to recognize you. Momentum builds quietly.

Consistency also builds trust. When readers see you show up week after week, book after book, they begin to believe in your staying power. And readers invest emotionally in authors who appear committed to the long haul.

Virality is unpredictable. Consistency is controllable.

Successful indie authors choose what they can control.

They understand that showing up 100 times in a small way often produces more cumulative impact than showing up once in a big way.

The compound effect of steady output—new releases, newsletters, thoughtful social media posts—outperforms the rollercoaster of chasing trends.

Instead of asking, "How do I go viral?" they ask, "How do I build a rhythm I can maintain?"

That question changes the trajectory of a career.

Visibility Over Perfection

Perfection is one of the most expensive habits an indie author can maintain.

Many writers delay publishing delay posting, delay pitching, and delay launching because they are trying to refine everything to a flawless state. They tweak cover designs endlessly. They rewrite back cover copy twenty times. They hesitate to share behind-the-scenes content because it does not feel polished enough.

Meanwhile, successful indie authors are visible.

Visibility does not mean sloppiness. It means understanding that clarity and connection matter more than cosmetic perfection. It means recognizing that readers respond to authenticity, consistency, and value—not to unattainable standards.

Perfectionism often masquerades as professionalism. But in practice, it can become procrastination.

Indie authors who sell steadily are willing to publish when the book is professionally edited and thoughtfully prepared—but not endlessly delayed.

They are willing to post content that is helpful and genuine—even if it is not award-winning prose.

They are willing to experiment publicly, test new ideas, and refine as they go.

Visibility creates opportunity. Perfection creates hesitation.

The marketplace rewards authors who participate. If readers cannot see you, they cannot buy from you.

If you are waiting for flawless execution before speaking up, you are competing against authors who are already building relationships in real time.

Progress invites growth. Silence does not.

Why "Quiet" Authors Often Sell More

There is a persistent myth that the loudest authors sell the most books. Social media can reinforce this illusion. It is easy to equate high visibility with high revenue.

But many of the most financially stable indie authors operate quietly.

They are not constantly announcing their word counts. They are not live-streaming every writing session. They are not engaging in daily debates about industry trends. Instead, they are writing. Publishing. Building backlists. Communicating consistently with their readers. Refining their craft.

Their growth is often steady rather than dramatic.

"Quiet" authors focus on infrastructure. They build email lists. They create reader magnets. They write series that encourage read-through. They invest in professional covers and editing. They treat each book as a long-term asset rather than a one-time event. Because they are not chasing noise, they are building depth. Depth converts.

A strong backlist means that every new release lifts previous titles. A nurtured email list means that each launch starts with built-in momentum. A clear brand means readers know exactly what they will receive.

Quiet does not mean invisible. It means focused.

These authors are not distracted by every new platform or trending strategy. They evaluate opportunities strategically. They understand that sustained output in one clear direction often outperforms scattered effort across many.

While others are chasing attention, they are building catalogs.

And catalogs sell.

Playing the Long Game Without Losing Motivation

The long game sounds noble in theory. In practice, it can feel slow.

Publishing consistently without immediate dramatic results requires emotional endurance. It requires believe in processes that may take years to fully mature. It requires resilience when early launches are modest and audience growth feels incremental.

Successful indie authors stay motivated because they measure differently.

Instead of focusing solely on daily sales numbers, they track long-term metrics: catalog growth, reader retention, list expansion, read-through rates. They celebrate milestones such as completing a series, improving conversion rates, or hitting consistent monthly income targets—even if those numbers are not flashy.

They understand that momentum compounds across releases. The first book may struggle. The third performs better. The sixth benefits from everything that came before it.

Motivation grows when you see progress, not just peaks.

Playing the long game also requires intentional mindset work. You must detach from comparison. There will always be authors who appear to move faster. But sustainable success is not a race; it is alignment between output and capacity.

When your publishing pace matches your real life, when your promotion system fits your energy, when your goals reflect your season, motivation becomes steadier.

You are not constantly trying to catch up. You are building forward.

The long game rewards patience—but only if patience is paired with action. Quiet, repeated action. Book after book. Month after month.

Action Steps: Adopt the Habits of Successful Indie Authors

1. **Choose a Consistent Visibility Rhythm:** Decide how often you will show up publicly—through newsletters, social media, blog posts, or other channels—and commit to a schedule you can sustain for at least six months. Consistency beats bursts of activity every time.

2. **Publish When Ready, Not When Perfect:** Identify one area where perfectionism has delayed progress. Set a clear completion standard and move forward once it's met. Progress fuels momentum; perfection often stalls it.

3. **Strengthen Your Infrastructure:** If you don't have an email list, start building one. If you already have a list, create a plan to nurture it consistently. Focus on assets that grow over time, not just short-term attention.

4. **Track Long-Term Metrics:** Shift focus from daily fluctuations to quarterly progress. Monitor catalog size, subscriber growth, and release consistency. This perspective helps you make strategic decisions rather than reactive ones.

5. **Define Your Three-Year Vision:** Write down where you want your author career to be in three years. Then ask yourself, which consistent actions, if repeated, would make that outcome likely?

<u>Key Takeaway:</u> Successful indie authors aren't necessarily louder, luckier, or more talented—they are **steadier**. The prioritize consistency over virality, visibility over perfection, depth over noise, and endurance over urgency. Over time, these habits compound into a career built on momentum, not fleeting moments.

Conclusion

Promotion Is Ongoing—But It Gets Easier

If you take nothing else from this book, take this: promotion is not an event. It is an ongoing rhythm. And while that may sound exhausting at first, it is actually freeing.

Because once you understand that promotion never truly ends, you stop waiting for it to feel finished.

There is not magical week when you can finally say, "Now I'm done promoting." There is no single campaign that permanently solves visibility.

Promotion is woven into the fabric of an author career. It evolves. It stretches. It adapts. But it does not disappear.

The good news?

It gets easier.

Not because the work vanishes. But because you grow into it.

You develop systems. You refine your message. You understand your audience more clearly. You stop overcomplicating what works. You learn what to ignore.

And with each book, each launch, each season, you gain data, resilience, and confidence.

The panic fades. The process strengthens.

Redefining Success Beyond Launch Week

One of the most harmful myths in the indie space is the idea that launch week determines a book's fate. It does not.

Launch week is important, yes. It is an opportunity to generate momentum, activate your email list, and remind your audience that you exist. But it is not a final verdict on your book's potential.

Too many authors emotionally tie their sense of success to seven days.

If sales are high, they feel validated. If sales are modest, they feel defeated.

This narrow definition of success creates unnecessary discouragement.

A book is not a product with a one-week lifespan. It is an asset. It can sell for years. It can find new audiences months later. It can be revitalized through promotions, series additions, updated covers, or simply a larger catalog.

Success must be measured beyond the launch window.

Ask better questions:

- Did I grow my email list during this launch?

- Did I improve my systems compared to my last release?

- Did I strengthen relationships with my readers?

- Did I complete another book and add it to my catalog?

These are indicators of long-term health.

When you redefine success as forward motion instead of immediate volume, you remove the emotional volatility that derails so many writers. You begin to see each release not as a final exam, but as another step in a cumulative journey.

And that perspective changes everything.

Why Every Book Makes the Next One Easier to Sell

At the beginning of your career, promotion feels disproportionately heavy.

You have one book. One link. One entry point for readers. Every sale requires effort. Every reader must be persuaded from scratch.

But something powerful happens as your catalog grows.

Each book becomes a marketing asset for the others.

When you release your second book, readers who discover it may go back and purchase the first. When you publish a third, you increase your chances of read-through. When you write within a series or consistent genre, you create momentum that multiplies.

Selling one book is difficult. Selling a catalog is strategic.

Your backlist does part of the promotional work for you. A reader who enjoys one title may purchase three more without additional advertising. A new subscriber who joins your list has multiple options to explore. A promotion for one book can create ripple effects across your entire body of work.

This is why ongoing writing matters so much.

Each finished manuscript is not just a creative accomplishment. It is an additional doorway into your author brand. It increases discoverability. It deepens trust. It gives readers more reasons to stay.

Early in your journey, effort feels heavy because infrastructure is minimal. Later, effort becomes more efficient because your foundation is stronger.

The first book builds courage.

The second builds credibility.

The third begins to build leverage.

Over time, your catalog becomes your greatest promotional tool.

A Little Encouragement for Those of You Who Feel Behind

If you are reading this and quietly wondering whether you're behind, I want you to sit with that feeling for a moment—not to dwell in it, but to examine it gently. Behind compared to whom? Behind according to what timeline? Behind by whose definition of success?

One of the most subtle dangers in the indie author world is the constant exposure to other people's milestones. You see book deal announcements, rapid release schedules, screenshots of impressive sales dashboards, growing social media followings, and packed launch teams. Because these highlights are visible, they begin to feel like a standard. Without realizing it, you measure your private, day-to-day effort against someone else's curated peak moments.

That comparison distorts reality.

Every author's life circumstances are different. Some writers are building their careers with flexible schedules, financial backing, or fewer personal obligations. Others are writing in the margins—early mornings before work, late nights after children are asleep, weekends carved out between responsibilities. Some are navigating health challenges, relocations, caregiving roles, or demanding careers alongside their creative ambitions. Progress achieved under constraint is not lesser progress. In many cases, it reflects greater resilience.

It is also important to recognize that visible speed does not always equal sustainable success. Rapid growth can be thrilling, but it can also be fragile. A fast release schedule without strong systems can lead to burnout. A large audience without clear branding can dilute long-term engagement. A spike in sales without infrastructure can fade just as quickly as it arrived.

Slow growth, when built intentionally, often proves stronger.

If your journey feels steady instead of explosive, that does not mean you are failing. It may mean you are building something that will last. Each book you finish strengthens your craft. Each launch you execute improves your process. Each reader who joins your email list—whether one or one hundred—represents a real person choosing to connect with your work.

Those small numbers matter.

Momentum in publishing is cumulative, not immediate. The author with a thriving catalog today once started at a dashboard that showed single-digit sales. The writer who now confidently launches a series once doubted whether anyone would read their first chapter.

They were not ahead. They were simply earlier in the process of compounding.

If you feel behind, I encourage you to shift your focus from pace to direction. Are you moving forward? Are you writing? Are you learning? Are you refining your systems? If the answer is yes, then you are not stuck—you are progressing. The speed may vary from season to season, but forward is forward.

There will be times in your life when output slows. Responsibilities increase. Energy shifts. Priorities evolve. That does not invalidate what you have built. It simply means your career is unfolding within the context of a full life. And a full life is not an obstacle to your author journey—it is the very source of depth and experience that enriches your writing.

Be cautious about measuring your beginning against someone else's middle. What you see publicly is rarely the whole story. Years of quiet effort often precede visible success. Systems are built behind the scenes. Skills are sharpened in obscurity. Confidence grows through repetition, not applause.

Instead of asking, "Why am I not further along?" consider asking, "What is the next right step for me in this season?" That question is grounding.

It brings your focus back to what you can control today rather than what someone else accomplished yesterday.

Your timeline does not need to match anyone else's to be valid. What matters is sustainability. What matters is alignment between your goals and your capacity. What matters is continuing to move forward in a way that allows you to keep going next year—and the year after that.

You are not behind. You are building.

And building—when done thoughtfully and consistently—always takes time.

READY. SET. PROMOTE!

References

Professional Book Publishing Coaching

Goldspiel Creative Enterprises: https://goldspielcreativeenterprises.com/services/done-with-you-self-publishing/

ARC, Review, and Launch Team Building

BookSprout (collect Advance Reader Copies (ARCs) and obtain early reviews): https://booksprout.co/

Book Bounty (secure book reviews): https://book-bounty.com/

Pubby (secure book reviews): https://app.pubby.co/

Social Media Management

Content 360 (social media scheduler): https://get.content360.io/

Meet Edgar (social media scheduler): https://meetedgar.com/

Later (social media scheduler): https://later.com

Buffer (social media scheduler): https://buffer.com/

Hootsuite: https://www.hootsuite.com/

Email Building

Kit (email service provider – affiliate link): https://partners.kit.com/h60u79go7yf2

Mailchimp: https://mailchimp.com

MailerLite: https://www.mailerlite.com/

Constant Contact: https://www.constantcontact.com/

Categories, Keywords, and Discoverability

Publisher Rocket (formerly KDP Rocket – affiliate link): https://publisherrocket.cartknox.com/buy-rocket?aff=476

Best Seller Ranking Pro (Lifetime Membership – affiliate link): https://vgold_bestsellerrankingpro--tckpublishing.thrivecart.com/bestseller-ranking-pro-special-lifetime/

Reader Platforms

Goodreads: https://www.goodreads.com/

BookBub Author Profile: https://partners.bookbub.com/users/sign_up

Amazon Author Central: https://author.amazon.com/

Ad Platforms

Amazon Ads: https://advertising.amazon.com/

BookBub Ads: https://www.bookbub.com/partners/bookbub_ads

Book Promoters

Written Word Media: https://secure.writtenwordmedia.com/features

Robin Reads: https://robinreads.com/nonfiction-paid/

Fussy Librarian: https://www.thefussylibrarian.com/advertising/making-book-marketing-easier

Bargain Booksy: https://www.bargainbooksy.com/sell-more-books/

Ereader News Today: https://www.ereadernewstoday.com/bargain-and-free-book-submissions/

Ereader IQ: https://www.ereaderiq.com/authors/submissions/dds

Many Books: https://manybooks.net/get-featured

Book Gorilla: https://www.bookgorilla.com/advertise

Book Sends: https://booksends.com/advertise.php

The Ereader Café: https://theereadercafe.com/sell-more-books/

Please Do Me A Huge Favor

I f ***Ready, Set, Promote: The Essential Marketing and Selling Guide for Self-Published Authors*** has helped you market your book with more clarity and confidence, I would be sincerely grateful for your support.

Your feedback not only helps me continue creating practical marketing resources for authors—it also helps other writers find a guide they can trust as they work to grow their visibility, reach more readers, and sell more books.

Here are a few meaningful ways you can support this book and help more authors get their work seen:

Write an Amazon review: Reviews play a powerful role in helping books get discovered. A brief, honest review not only supports this book—it helps other authors decide if this marketing guide is the right fit for them.

Recommend or gift this book: Know an author who's struggling to market their book or gain traction? Sharing or gifting this guide can give them the clarity and direction they need to start reaching readers.

Share your biggest takeaway: If something in this book clicked for you, share it on X, Facebook, Instagram, LinkedIn, or your favorite platform along with a link to the book. Even a quick post can help another author discover the strategies they've been missing.

You can find my **Amazon Author Page here:** https://www.amazon.co m/stores/Veronica-Goldspiel/author/B0D466HRG9

To join my **Private Face-book Group for Writers and Authors, click here:** https://www.face-book.com/groups/fromwritertoauthoraselfpub lishingsuccesscommunity

To sign-up for my **From Writer To Author Weekly NEWSLETTER, click here:** https://goldspiel-creative-enterprises.kit.com/newsletter

Check out the **From Writer To Author: The Podcast** here: https://fr omwritertoauthorthepodcast.buzzsprout.com/

A Special Discount Just for My Readers

You wrote your book. You published it. You did the hard part. So why isn't it getting the attention it deserves?

Before you start second-guessing everything, here's the truth: **It's usually not your book—it's how it's positioned.**

The Deep Dive Book Audit

A clear, strategic review of your book's Amazon presence and reader experience—so you know exactly what's helping, what's hurting, and what to fix first.

How It Works

This is not a Zoom call. No scheduling. No pressure.

You'll receive:
- A private recorded video walkthrough of your book and listing
- A detailed email report + prioritized action plan
-

Watch it on your time, revisit it anytime, and take action with confidence.

What I Review
- Amazon listing (title, description, cover, pricing)
- Visibility (keywords, categories, positioning)
- Author Central page
- Inside your book (formatting, flow, calls-to-action)

Why It Matters
Small issues can quietly cost you clicks, sales, and reviews. This audit shows you exactly where those issues are— and how to fix them without overwhelm.

Your Reader-Only Offer
Take **$100 OFF** your Deep Dive Book Audit
Use code: **RSPromote100** at checkout.

Ready to Stop Guessing?

If your book should be doing better... let's make sure nothing is holding it back.

Book your Deep Dive Book Audit today:
https://goldspielcreativeenterprises.com/deep-dive-book-audit/

About The Author

 Veronica Goldspiel is a bestselling author, book coach, editor, and publishing professional who helps aspiring and self-published authors turn their ideas into professionally published books. With years of experience working with writers and creatives, she is known for breaking down complex publishing and marketing concepts into clear, practical steps authors can actually use.

Before launching her work in the independent publishing world, Veronica spent nearly two decades working as an independent contractor with companies founded by Tony Robbins, where she gained extensive experience in business operations, content development, and supporting entrepreneurs and thought leaders. That background shaped her practical, results-focused approach to helping authors build successful publishing paths.

Veronica is the author of multiple nonfiction books focused on writing, self-publishing, marketing, freelancing, and personal growth. Her straightforward, no-nonsense style has made her a trusted resource for writers who want real-world guidance without unnecessary jargon or complicated marketing theories.

In addition to writing, Veronica provides professional book editing, formatting, and publishing support through her creative business, helping authors produce high-quality books that stand confidently in today's competitive marketplace. She also shares insights and advice for writers through her podcast, From Writer to Author: The Podcast, where she discusses the realities of writing, publishing, and building a sustainable author career.

Through her books, courses, and coaching, Veronica focuses on one core belief: authors deserve straightforward information that empowers them to make smart decisions about their writing and publishing journey. Her work emphasizes practical strategies, ethical publishing practices, and long-term career thinking rather than quick shortcuts or expensive gimmicks.

Ready, Set, Promote! continues her mission to help independent authors understand that publishing a book is only the beginning. With the right knowledge and consistent effort, any author can learn how to connect their book with the readers who are looking for it.

When she's not writing, editing, or teaching authors, Veronica enjoys creative pursuits like music, crafting, and exploring new ideas for her next book.

Visit: ***GoldspielCreativeEnterprises.com***

Other Books By The Author

Ready, Set, Publish: The Essential Pre-Publishing Roadmap for First-Time Authors (Book 1 of the Writers and Authors Series)

154 Fun Things To Do In Retirement From Home: Fun Hobbies, Adventures, and Cool Bucket List Ideas for the Elderly, Homebound, or Just Plain Anti-Social (Book 3 of the Retirement Series)

130+ Fun Things To Do In Retirement For Women: Fun, Feminine, and Fabulous Hobbies, Adventures, and Cool Bucket List Ideas To Make Retirement Your Best Chapter Yet (Book 2 of the Retirement Series)

151 Fun Things To Do In Retirement: Exciting Hobbies, Adventures, And Cool Bucket List Ideas To Make Retirement Your Best Chapter Yet (Book 1 of the Retirement Series)

Engage and Thrive: A Guide to Building a Strong Online Community of Raving Fans (Book 2 of the Small Business Wealth Marketing Series)

Finance For Freelancers: Maximize Income, Manage Cash Flow, Minimize Stress (Book 2 of The Freelancer's Life Series)

Freelance Success Secrets: 21 Essential Habits That Will Transform Your Freelance Business From Surviving To Thriving (Book 1 of The Freelancer's Life Series)

Reflections for Dream Catchers: The Inspirational Book of Wisdom for Your Journey to Success (Book 2 of the Personal Growth and Motivational Series)

Dream Catchers: Mastering the Art of Realizing Your Dreams (Book 1 of the Personal Growth and Motivational Series)

From Likes to Profits: A Guide to Choosing the Most Profitable Social Media Platforms for Your Brand (Book 1 of the Small Business Wealth Marketing Series)

Making Your Business a Social Media Superstar: The Step-by-Step Guide to Creating, Maintaining, and Promoting Your Online Presence (as Veronica Buhl)